George Whitefield.

Classics of Reformed Spirituality

"To honour God"
The spirituality of Oliver Cromwell
Michael A.G. Haykin

The revived Puritan
The spirituality of George Whitefield
Michael A.G. Haykin

Forthcoming

Jonathan Edwards on revival
Selections from the sermons of Alexander Whyte
The hymns of Ann Griffiths
Selections from Anne Steele and Benjamin Beddome
The spirituality of Thomas Boston
The spirituality of Philip Doddridge
The diary of Joseph Williams

Michael A.G. Haykin, series editor

Classics of Reformed Spirituality

The revived Puritan

The spirituality of George Whitefield

Edited and introduced by
Michael A.G. Haykin

Foreword by
John H. Armstrong

press

Dundas, Ontario

Joshua Press Inc.,
Dundas, Ontario, Canada
fax 905.627.8451
www.joshuapress.com

© 2000 by Joshua Press Inc.

Editorial director: Michael A.G. Haykin
Creative/production manager: Janice Van Eck

© Cover illustration by Deborah Livingston-Lowe
© Cover design by Janice Van Eck

Frontispiece is an engraving of George Whitefield based on
the portrait by Nathaniel Hone.

Canadian Cataloguing in Publication Data

Whitefield, George, 1714–1770
    The revived Puritan: the spirituality of George Whitefield

(Classics of Reformed spirituality)
Includes bibliographical references.
ISBN 1-894400-06-2

1. Whitefield, George, 1714–1770 — Contributions to
spirituality. 2. Spirituality — Methodist Church — History
— 18th century.   I. Haykin, Michael A.G.   II. Title.
III. Series

BX9225.W4A25 2000   248'.092   C00-931280-3

To the memory of Arnold A. Dallimore (1911–1998),
learned biographer and friend,
who made the life and doctrine of Whitefield
speak to a new generation,
and to May E. Dallimore,
his faithful wife and friend.

Contents

13
Foreword

17
Acknowledgements

21
The revived Puritan:
The spirituality of George Whitefield

79
Chronology

83
Selections from George Whitefield's
letters and prayers

223
Appendix

229
Endnotes

249
Select bibliography

253
Reading spiritual classics

1738

God give me a deep humility, a well-guided zeal,
a burning love, and a single eye,
and let men or devils do their worst.

1749

Was [the Apostle Paul] not filled with a holy restless
Impatience and insatiable Thirst of travelling,
and undertaking dangerous Voyages
for the Conversion of infidels...?

1749

If any of my poor writings have been blessed to any,
let Christ have the glory...

—George Whitefield

Foreword

In an age when spirituality is exalted through non-evangelical traditions, it is imperative that we have models, of the most practical sort, of the relationship between sound doctrine and personal piety. Michael Haykin has provided us with such a model in *The revived Puritan: The spirituality of George Whitefield*, showing how the obvious personal piety and deep spirituality of George Whitefield is clearly revealed in his letters.

George Whitefield has been variously interpreted and misunderstood by biographers. Some have seen, in his dramatic style of preaching, an orator who moved masses of people simply by the magnetism and force of his style. His pulpit powers were, to say the least, noteworthy. His voice and manner were the envy of contemporary English actors. The famous actor David Garrick once noted that Whitefield could prompt his hearers to weep or rejoice by how he pronounced the word "Mesopotamia." Whitefield's pathos and earnest manner were undoubtedly profound. But to ground his amazing public ministry merely in these gifts is a huge mistake. Haykin's wonderfully written Introduction, and the selected letters that follow, will plainly show why this thesis regarding Whitefield's ministry cannot be accurate.

George Whitefield was pre-eminently a Christ-centered man. He was a deeply spiritual and immensely earnest individual who harnessed his obvious talent for the service of the Christ he profoundly loved. No careful reading of these letters will leave any other impression. Whitefield was, in the best sense of the term, a reformational revivalist. He was experientially rooted in the great doctrinal themes recovered by the sixteenth-century Reformers, as Haykin's Introduction plainly demonstrates. He was also a passionate communicator of the simple truths of the gospel who sought to bring his hearers to deeper love for Christ, either by means of the new birth and conversion or by increasing personal zeal for the person and work of Christ among true believers.

Whitefield made several obvious mistakes, especially early in his ministry. These must not be glossed over. Yet, the true record will plainly demonstrate that he eventually became the most effective preacher of his time, precisely because of his deep personal humility, his studied and developed piety, and his faithful use of God-given opportunities.

The late Arnold Dallimore gave this generation a marvellous gift in his biographical treatment of Whitefield. Michael Haykin has now given us an extremely important new work that will serve to focus our thoughts more directly upon the precise reasons why God was pleased to singularly use this wonderful man. If you have already read Dallimore you will profit from this little book. If you have not yet read Dallimore read Michael Haykin's wonderful Introduction first. The particular letters chosen for this volume are both revealing and reflective. Several of them moved me personally to tears and earnest prayer for more of Christ's love and presence in my own life. There is far too little of this kind of piety to be found in our day. May God give this invaluable little book a large place in the life of the modern church. If we are to see true revival again we will need material such as this to fan true flames into Christ-centered holiness.

John H. Armstrong
Carol Stream, Illinois
February 2000

George Whitefield

[From an engraving by J. Hopwood. Now in the author's possession.]

Acknowledgements

My first exposure to the Evangelical literature of the eighteenth century was in the late 1970s and it was basically centred on the treatises and letters of John Wesley. His boldness and his theological vision captured my thoughts at that time and I must admit that his friend and co-worker, George Whitefield, received short shrift. However, all of this changed in 1982 when I was given Dr. Arnold Dallimore's two-volume biography of Whitefield as a graduation present. Dallimore's clear desire to rehabilitate Whitefield and restore him to his rightful place in the annals of eighteenth-century church history awakened me to a chapter of the eighteenth century I had largely overlooked. In a sense, then, this book has its roots in Dallimore's marvellous account of Whitefield's life and ministry. The gift of these two volumes also helped me towards the embrace of Calvinistic theology and spirituality, which I today regard as the best expression of biblical theology and spirituality.

Little did I think then, though, that I would one day write a book on Whitefield. My indebtedness in the writing of this work is wide and varied. Pastor Leigh Powell helped enormously in loaning me his 1771 three-volume edition of Whitefield's letters, a set that is quite difficult to locate. The typing of the letters chosen for inclusion in this volume went smoothly with the able assistance of Marina Coldwell and Ruth Engler. May Dallimore, the wife of Dr. Dallimore, gave me some of her late husband's notes and papers on Whitefield, which proved to be invaluable. For advice and encouragement at various stages of the book I am also grateful to Pierre Tellier, S. Gregory Fields, Dr. Mike Renihan, Dr. Joel Beeke, Dr. Ruth E. Mayers and Sue Mills, the librarian/archivist of the Angus Library, Regent's Park College, Oxford University. Two other librarians that must be mentioned for their provision of vital assistance are Rev. Ron Kilpatrick, the librarian of Knox Theological Seminary, Fort Lauderdale, and Marion Meadows, the librarian of the seminary at which I regularly teach, Heritage Theological Seminary in Cambridge, Ontario. The McMaster University Archives and Research Collections, with its emphasis on eighteenth-century English imprints, was also a great help in my locating some Whitefield titles.

With regard to the actual production of this book I am extremely grateful to Deborah Livingston-Lowe for her art-work that adorns the cover and to Janice Van Eck for her indispensable expertise in the layout and design of the book. Finally I would like to thank Dr. John Armstrong for writing the "Foreword." The friendship that lies behind his words means a great deal to me.

The inspiration for the title of this book lies in a reference in J.I. Packer's essay on Whitefield's spirituality to an 1829 book of selections from Whitefield's works called *The Revived Puritan*. As Packer remarks, this phrase is "uncannily apt" as a description of the evangelist.[1] The subtitle is modelled on Frank Baker's *Charles Wesley As Revealed by His Letters*.[2]

Editing of the letters and prayers included in this volume has been kept to a minimum. Idiosyncracies of eighteenth-century typography, such as the use of capitals and italics, have been changed to bring the text into line with twenty-first century usage. On occasion there have been changes in the punctuation to make the text more readable. Where possible the recipients of Whitefield's letters have been identified. One final point has to do with the process by which letters were selected for inclusion in this volume. They have been chosen primarily with a view to illustrating the major themes of Whitefield's piety. This explains why there are so few letters from his final years, something that would not be acceptable if we were seeking to use his letters to outline his life.

Dundas, Ontario
February, 2000

---

[1] "The Spirit with the Word: The Reformational Revivalism of George Whitefield" in W.P. Stephens, ed., *The Bible, the Reformation and the Church. Essays in Honour of James Atkinson* (*Journal for the Study of the New Testament Supplement Series* 105; Sheffield: Sheffield Academic Press, 1995), 176 and n.33.

[2] *Charles Wesley As Revealed by His Letters* (London: The Epworth Press, 1948).

First Presbyterian Church, Newburyport, Massachusetts

[From a lithograph by W.S. Barlett. Now in the author's possession.]

The revived Puritan: The spirituality of George Whitefield

In 1835 Francis Alexander Cox (1783–1853) and James Hoby (1788–1871), two prominent English Baptists who were visiting fellow Baptists in the United States, made a side trip to Newburyport, Massachusetts, to view the tomb of George Whitefield (1714–1770). The "grand itinerant" had died on September 30, 1770, at the home of Jonathan Parsons (1705–1776), pastor of the town's First Presbyterian Church, also known as Old South. He had been interred two days later in a vault below what is now the centre aisle of this church, where, along with the coffins of Parsons and another pastor of the church, Joseph Prince (d.1791), his remains were on display all through the nineteenth century. In fact, it was not until 1932 that the coffin in which Whitefield's remains lay was covered over with a slate slab.[1]*

Cox and Hoby later recalled descending with some difficulty into the subterranean vault where

* For endnotes, see page 229.

Whitefield was buried. As they did so, they remembered that "deep expectant emotions thrilled our bosoms." They sat on the two other coffins in the vault and watched as the upper half of the lid of Whitefield's coffin was opened on its hinges "to reveal the skeleton secrets of the narrow prison-house." They "contemplated and handled the skull," while they "thought of his devoted life, his blessed death, his high and happy destiny" and "whispered [their] adorations of the grace that formed him both for earth and heaven."[2] What makes this scene even more *outré* is that the skeletal remains that Cox and Hoby viewed were not intact. The main bone of Whitefield's right arm had been stolen some years earlier by another Englishman. It was not until either the late 1830s or even the 1840s that the thief's conscience brought him to the point of sending the bone back across the Atlantic in a small wooden box![3]

These accounts are a potent reminder of the fact that of all the great preachers raised up in the transatlantic Evangelical Revival none gripped the public mind and imagination more than George Whitefield. During his lifetime, the Congregationalist Joseph Williams (1692–1755), a merchant from Kidderminster with a keen interest in spiritual renewal, rightly termed him the "Father" of those seeking to advance the revival.[4] Henry St. John, Viscount Bolingbroke (1678–1751), who "professed himself a deist," was forced to exclaim, after hearing Whitefield preach: "the most extraordinary man of our times, the most commanding eloquence, unquenchable zeal, unquestionable piety."[5] On the other side of the Atlantic Benjamin Colman (1673–1747) and William Cooper (1694–1743) viewed Whitefield as "the wonder of the age" and were convinced that "no man more employs the pens, and fills up the conversation of people, than he does at this day."[6] Shortly after the evangelist's death Augustus Montague Toplady (1740–1778), author of the famous hymn "Rock of Ages, cleft for me," remembered him as "the apostle of the English empire."[7] And looking back from the following century, John Foster (1770–1843), the Baptist essayist, was sure that with "the doubtful exception of Wickliffe, no man probably ever excited in this island [i.e. the British Isles] so profound, and extended, and prolonged a sensation in the public mind, by personal addresses to the understanding and conscience, on the subject of religion."[8]

"A ray of divine life": *The pathway to conversion*[9]

Whitefield was the youngest son of Thomas Whitefield (1681–1716), the proprietor of the Bell Inn, at the time the finest hotel in Gloucester. George's father died when he was but two and so he was raised by his mother Elizabeth (c.1681–1751). His school record was unremarkable, save for a noticeable talent for acting. For a while during his teen years, when his older brother Richard took over the running of the inn, he worked as one of the servants. But his mother longed for something better for her son. Her persistence and the kindness of friends enabled him in November 1732 to enter Pembroke College, Oxford University. It was here in the following summer that he first met John Wesley (1703–1791) and his younger brother Charles (1707–1788), who were regularly meeting with a group of men known to history as "the Holy Club." This was a company of ten or so men who were ardently trying to live religious lives in an extremely dissolute age.

Whitefield, like-minded and longing for spiritual companionship ever since coming up to Oxford, joined them. He engaged in numerous religious exercises, such as fasting, praying regularly, attending public worship, and seeking to abstain from what were deemed worldly pleasures. Systematic reading of Puritan and Pietist devotional literature also occupied much of Whitefield's time.[10] Despite the evident zeal he brought to these religious activities he had no sense of peace with God or that God was satisfied with what he was doing. He was, though he did not know it at the time, treading a pathway similar to the one that Martin Luther (1483–1546) had taken over two hundred years earlier. And just as Luther's conversion was the spark that lit the fires of the Reformation, so Whitefield's conversion would be central to kindling the blaze of the eighteenth-century Evangelical Revival.[11]

Conversion came in the spring of 1735 after Charles Wesley had given him a copy of *The Life of God in the Soul of Man* (1677) by Henry Scougal (1650–1678), a former Professor of Divinity at Aberdeen.[12] This book was a frontal challenge to Whitefield's ardent endeavour to create a righteous life that would merit God's favour. Here is the way Whitefield recalled it many years later in a sermon that he preached in 1769:

I must bear testimony to my old friend Mr. Charles Wesley, he put a book into my hands, called, *The Life of God in the Soul of Man*, whereby God shewed me, that I must be born again, or be damned. I know the place: it may be superstitious, perhaps, but whenever I go to Oxford, I cannot help running to that place where Jesus Christ first revealed himself to me, and gave me the new birth. As a good writer [i.e. Scougal] says, a man may go to church, say his prayers, receive the Sacrament, and yet, my brethren, not be a Christian. How did my heart rise, how did my heart shudder, like a poor man that is afraid to look into his account-books, lest he should find himself a bankrupt: yet shall I burn that book, shall I throw it down, shall I put it by, or shall I search into it? I did [search it], and, holding the book in my hand, thus addressed the God of heaven and earth: Lord, if I am not a Christian, if I am not a real one, for Jesus Christ's sake, shew me what Christianity is, that I may not be damned at last. I read a little further, and the cheat was discovered; O, says the author, they that know any thing of religion know it is a vital union with the Son of God, Christ formed in the heart; O what a ray of divine life did then break in upon my poor soul...[13]

Awakened by this book to his need for the new birth, Whitefield passionately struggled to find salvation along the pathway of extreme asceticism but to no avail. Finally, when he had come to an end of his resources as a human being, God enabled him, in his words, "to lay hold on His dear Son by a living faith, and, by giving me the Spirit of adoption, to seal me, as I humbly hope, even to the day of everlasting redemption." And, he went on, "oh! with what joy—joy unspeakable—even joy that was full of, and big with glory, was my soul filled..."[14]

"The open bracing air": The life of a preacher

Always the avid reader, it was Whitefield's prayerful perusal of the Puritan biblical commentaries of William Burkitt (1650–1703) and Matthew Henry (1662–1714) a few months after his conversion that led to his becoming convinced of "free grace and the necessity of being justified in His [i.e. God's] sight by *faith only*."[15] After his ordination as deacon in the Church of England the following year, these

Reformation doctrines came to occupy a central place in his preaching arsenal.[16] There is, for instance, a recently published account of Whitefield's preaching drawn up by an unknown French contemporary, dated August 1739. This observer states that Whitefield preaches "continually about inner regeneration, the new birth in Jesus Christ, the movement of the Spirit, justification by faith through grace [*justification par la foy de grace*], the life of the Spirit."[17]

The following year Joseph Smith, a Congregationalist minister from Charleston, South Carolina, defended Whitefield against various attacks in *The Character, Preaching, etc. of the Rev. George Whitefield*.[18] In the section dealing with the doctrinal content of Whitefield's sermons, Smith lists four "primitive, protestant, puritanic" doctrines that Whitefield regularly heralded in his preaching in America—original sin, justification by faith alone, the new birth and inward feelings of the Spirit.[19] Smith recalled the way in which Whitefield

> earnestly contended for our justification as the free gift of God, by faith alone in the blood of Christ, an article of faith delivered to the saints of old...telling us plainly, and with the clearest distinction, that a man was justified these three ways; meritoriously by Christ, instrumentally by faith alone, declaratively by good works.[20]

Whitefield's preaching on the new birth was not

at all well received by the Anglican clergy in England, and churches began to be barred to him. By and large the bishops in the Hanoverian Church of England were, in the words of English historian J.H. Plumb, "first and foremost politicians," not men of the Spirit. "There is a worldliness," Plumb continues, "about eighteenth-century [bishops] which no amount of apologetics can conceal." They undertook their clerical duties "only as political duties allowed."[21] The worldliness of these bishops showed in other ways as well. Jonathan Trelawny (1650–1721), Bishop of Winchester, used to "excuse himself for his much swearing by saying he swore as a baronet, and not as a bishop!"[22] Such bishops had neither the time nor the interest to promote church renewal. Of course, the decadence of church leadership was by no means absolute; but the net effect of worldly bishops was to squash effective reform.

Moreover, the attention of far too many of the clergy under these bishops was taken up with such avocations as philosophy, biology, agriculture, chemistry, literature, law, politics, fox-hunting, drinking—anything but pastoral ministry and spiritual nurture. There were, of course, a goodly number of Church of England ministers who did not have the resources to indulge themselves in such pursuits, since they barely eked out a living. But few of them—wealthy or poor—preached anything but dry, unaffecting moralistic sermons. The *mentalité* of the first half of the eighteenth century gloried in reason, moderation and decorum. The preaching of the day dwelt largely upon themes of morality and decency and lacked "any element of holy excitement, of passionate pleading, of heroic challenge, of winged imagination."[23] Even among many of the churches of the Dissenters, the children of the Puritans, things were little better. One knowledgeable observer of these churches bemoaned the fact that "the distinguished doctrines of the gospel—Christ crucified, the only ground of hope for fallen man—salvation through his atoning blood—the sanctification by his eternal Spirit, are old-fashioned things now seldom heard in our churches."[24] The Christian life was basically defined in terms of a moral life of good works. Spiritual ardour was regarded with horror as "enthusiasm" or fanaticism. The ideal of the era is well summed up by an inscription on a tombstone from the period: "pious without enthusiasm."[25]

Whitefield, however, was not to be deterred. On Saturday, February 17, 1739, he made the decision to take to the open air and preach to a group of colliers in Kingswood, a coal-mining district on the outskirts of Bristol. These men with their families lived in squalor and utter degradation, squandering their lives in drink and violence. With no church nearby, they were quite ignorant of Christianity and its leading tenets. It was a key turning-point not only in his life but also in the history of Evangelicalism.[26] The concern that has gripped Evangelicals in the past two hundred years to bring the gospel message directly to ordinary people has some of its most significant roots here, in Whitefield's venturing out to preach in the open air.

From this point on, Whitefield would relish and delight in his calling as an open-air preacher. He would preach in fields and foundries, in ships, cemeteries, and pubs, atop horses and even a hangman's scaffold,[27] from stone walls and balconies, staircases and windmills.[28] For instance, referring to this calling, in a letter dated December 14, 1768, he wrote, "I love the open bracing air." And the following year he could state, "It is good to go into the high-ways and hedges. Field-preaching, field-preaching for ever!"[29]

It should be noted that Whitefield never confined his witnessing about Christ to preaching occasions. He took every opportunity to share his faith. "God forbid," he once remarked, "I should travel with anybody a quarter of an hour without speaking of Christ to them."[30] On another occasion, during his sixth preaching tour of America, he happened to stay with a wealthy, though worldly, family in Southold on Long Island. The family discovered after the evangelist had left their home that he had written with a diamond on one of the windowpanes in the bedroom where he had slept, "One thing is needful!"[31]

At that first open-air service in February of 1739 there were 200 people. Within six weeks or so, Whitefield was preaching numerous times a week to crowds sometimes numbering in the thousands![32] Whitefield's description of his ministry at this time is a classic one. To visualize the scene at the Kingswood collieries, we need to picture the green countryside, the piles of coal, the squalid huts and the deep semicircle of unwashed faces as we read his words:

Having no righteousness of their own to renounce, they were glad to hear of a Jesus who was a friend of publicans, and came not to call the righteous, but sinners to repentance. The first discovery of their being affected was to see the white gutters made by their tears which plentifully fell down their black cheeks, as they came out of their coal pits. Hundreds and hundreds of them were soon brought under deep convictions, which, as the event proved, happily ended in a sound and thorough conversion. The change was visible to all, though numbers chose to impute it to anything, rather than the finger of God.[33]

Here is another description from this same period of time, when others besides the miners of Bristol were flocking to hear Whitefield preach:

As...I had just begun to be an extempore preacher, it often occasioned many inward conflicts. Sometimes, when twenty thousand people were before me, I had not, in my own apprehension, a word to say either to God or them. But I never was totally deserted, and frequently...so assisted, that I knew by happy experience what our Lord meant by saying, "Out of his belly shall flow rivers of living water" (John 7:38). The open firmament above me, the prospect of the adjacent fields, with the sight of thousands and thousands, some in coaches, some on horseback, and some in the trees, and at times all affected and drenched in tears together, to which sometimes was added the solemnity of the approaching evening, was almost too much for, and quite overcame me.[34]

Revival had come to England! And to that revival, and its confluent streams in Wales, Scotland and British North America, no man contributed more than Whitefield. Over the 34 years between his conversion and death in 1770 in Newburyport, Massachusetts, it is calculated that he preached around 18,000 sermons.[35] Actually, if one includes all of the talks that he gave, he probably spoke about a thousand times a year during his ministry.[36] Moreover, many of his sermons were delivered to massive congregations that numbered 10,000 or so, some to audiences possibly as large as 20,000.[37]

In addition to his preaching throughout the length and breadth of England, he regularly itiner-ated throughout Wales, visited Ireland twice, and journeyed fourteen times to Scotland.[38] He crossed the Atlantic thirteen times, stopping once in Bermuda for eleven weeks, and preached in virtually every major town on the eastern seaboard of

America.[39] What is so remarkable about all of this is Whitefield lived at a time when travel to a town but twenty miles away was a significant undertaking.[40]

In journeying to Scotland and to America he was going to what many perceived as the fringes of transatlantic British society and culture.[41] And yet some of God's richest blessings on his ministry were in these very regions. For example, Harry Stout, commenting on Whitefield's impact on America, writes:

> So pervasive was Whitefield's impact in America that he can justly be styled America's first cultural hero. Before Whitefield, there was no unifying intercolonial person or event. Indeed, before Whitefield, it is doubtful any name other than royalty was known equally from Boston to Charleston. But by 1750 virtually every American loved and admired Whitefield and saw him as their champion.[42]

Whitefield's ministry—insisting, as it did, on the vital necessity of conversion and the work of the Holy Spirit in the heart[43]—was not without its critics, many of whom castigated him for what they regarded as fanaticism. In an interview with John Wesley on August 18, 1739, for example, Joseph Butler (1692–1752), the Bishop of Bristol, accused both Wesley and Whitefield of "pretending to extraordinary revelations and gifts of the Holy Ghost," which he found "a horrid thing—a very horrid thing."[44] Of course, if Whitefield had been present, he would have rightly disputed the accuracy of Butler's accusation.[45] John Callender (1706–1748), a Baptist pastor in Newport, Rhode Island, denounced Whitefield as "a second George Fox," obviously convinced, and wrongly so, that Whitefield, like the founder of the Quakers, publicly promoted the restoration of the extraordinary gifts of the Holy Spirit.[46]

It should be admitted that in his early ministry Whitefield did make some unguarded statements and adopted certain attitudes that helped fuel this opposition. On his second preaching tour of America, for instance, Whitefield appears to have maintained that assurance belonged to the essence of saving faith and that a mature Christian could discern the marks of conversion in another individual. As Jonathan Dickinson (1688–1747), the first president of the College of New Jersey (later known as Princeton University) and a friend to the revival, remarked about Whitefield's views at this time: "I cannot stand surety for all his Sentiments in Religion, particularly his making Assurance to be essentially necessary to a justifying Faith; And his openly declaring for a Spirit of discerning in experienced Christians, whereby they can know who are true converts, and who are close Hypocrites."[47] To his credit, Whitefield would later admit his injudiciousness and that he had been far "too rash and hasty" in his speech and published writings. "Wildfire has been mixed with it," he wrote in 1748, "and

I find that I frequently wrote and spoke in my own spirit, when I thought I was writing and speaking by the assistance of the Spirit of God."[48]

Despite these faults—basically overcome by his early thirties—multitudes of Whitefield's hearers found his preaching "moving, earnest, winning, melting" and rooted in a doctrinal framework which was "plainly that of the Reformers."[49] Sarah Edwards (1710–1758), the wife of the New England divine, Jonathan Edwards (1703–1758), was one such hearer. She heard Whitefield preach in her home church in Northampton, Massachusetts, a number of times between Friday, October 17 and Wednesday, October 22, 1741, when Whitefield left for New Haven and New York. Three days after Whitefield had left Northampton, Sarah, "an astute judge of pulpit manner,"[50] wrote to her brother, James Pierpoint, who lived in New Haven, to give him first-hand information about Whitefield.

I want to prepare you for a visit from the Rev. Mr. Whitefield, the famous preacher of England. He has been sojourning with us a week or more, and, after visiting a few of the neighbouring towns, is going to New Haven, and from thence to New York. He is truly a remarkable man, and during his visit has, I think, verified all that we have heard of him. He makes less of the doctrines [of grace] than our American preachers generally do, and aims more at affecting the heart. He is a born orator.

You have already heard of his deep-toned, yet clear and melodious voice. O it is perfect music to listen to that alone! And he speaks so easily, without any apparent effort. You remember that David Hume[51] thought it worth going twenty miles to hear him speak; and Garrick[52] said, 'He could move men to tears or make them tremble by his simple intonations in pronouncing the word Mesopotamia.' Well, this last was a mere speech of the play-actor; but it is truly wonderful to see what a spell this preacher often casts over an audience by proclaiming the simplest truths of the Bible. I have seen upward of a thousand people hang on his words with breathless silence, broken only by an occasional half-suppressed sob. He impresses the ignorant, and not less the educated and refined. It is reported, you know, that as the miners of England listened to him the tears made white furrows down their smutty cheeks, and so here our mechanics shut up their shops, and the day-labourers throw down their tools to go and hear him preach, and few go away unaffected. A prejudiced person, I know, might say that this is all theatrical artifice and display; but not so will any one think who has seen and known him. He is a very devout and godly man, and his only aim seems to be to reach and influence men the best way. He speaks from a heart all aglow with love, and pours out a torrent of eloquence which is almost irresistible. Many, very many persons in Northampton date the beginning of new thoughts, new desires, new purposes, and a new life, from the day on which they heard him preach of Christ and this salvation.[53]

J.I. Packer has drawn attention to at least three reasons mentioned in this letter for Whitefield's success as a preacher.[54] First, the Anglican evangelist addressed his hearers simply as fellow human beings, so that distinctions of rich and poor, educated and uneducated, ceased to matter. Whitefield spoke in such a way that he was readily understood and appreciated by the poor and uneducated as well as by the wealthy and learned.

Then, he put spiritual issues to his hearers as one who transparently loved them and longed for them to be delivered out of the bondage of sin. "He speaks from a heart all aglow with love," Sarah recalled. And many who came to mock the preacher and laugh at his doctrine went away sobered and ultimately converted as they heard of the love of God in Christ for sinners and felt that love through the medium of Whitefield's impassioned preaching. As we shall see, Whitefield was thoroughly convinced of what have been called the doctrines of grace, the distinguishing tenets of Calvinism. Yet, this never prevented him from giving "sweet invitations to close with Christ," which he considered to be "the very life of preaching."[55] Phillis Wheatley (1753–1784), the African-American poet, well cap-

Phillis Wheatley

[From Phillis Wheatley, *Poems on Various Subjects, Religious and Moral* (London, 1773), frontispiece]

tured Whitefield's passion in preaching, when, in her elegy on the evangelist, she wrote the following:

> That Saviour, which his soul did first receive,
> The greatest gift that ev'n a God can give,
> He freely offer'd to the num'rous throng,
> That on his lips with list'ning pleasure hung.
>
> "Take him, ye wretched, for your only good,
> Take him ye starving sinners, for your food;
> Ye thirsty, come to this life-giving stream,
> Ye preachers, take him for your joyful theme;
> Take him, my dear Americans, he said,
> Be your complaints on his kind bosom laid:
> Take him, ye Africans, he longs for you;
> Impartial Saviour is his title due:
> Wash'd in the fountain of redeeming blood,
> You shall be sons, and kings, and priests to
> God."[56]

Finally, Whitefield spoke as one who sought to awaken and grip the heart. In Sarah's words, he "aims...at affecting the heart." Unlike many of his Anglican contemporaries who addressed only the mind and whose preaching lacked zeal, Whitefield spoke to the whole man with passion and without mincing any words. In 1844, John Knight, an elderly man of eighty-one, recalled the time that he had heard Whitefield preach on the evangelist's final visit to Gloucestershire in 1769. According to Knight, he was "about 6 years of age" at the time. "My father held me up in his arms," he wrote, "and though so young I well remember to have seen the tears run down the cheek of that Servant of God while preaching the love of his Master to dying sinners."[57]

A fourth reason, not mentioned by Packer in these reflections on Sarah's fascinating letter, was Whitefield's godliness. Robert Philip was surely right when he wrote in his mid-nineteenth century biography of the evangelist that "the grand secret of Whitefield's power was…his devotional spirit."[58] To a consideration of that "devotional spirit" and piety we now turn.[59]

"The believer's hollow square": The new birth and justification by faith alone

Summing up the characteristics of transatlantic British society in the opening decades of the eighteenth century, Oxford historian John Walsh lists the following: a noticeable decay of ministerial authority, the growth of rationalism and a massive intellectual assault on supernatural Christianity, the spread of material wealth and "luxury," the frivolity of the young and an indifference on their part to spiritual matters and a sense of spiritual powerlessness among both pious Anglicans and Dissenters.[60] Attestation of this description is found in both public documents and private testimonies. Here is the witness of one author, the London Baptist theologian Benjamin

Keach (1640–1704), writing in 1701:

> Was ever sodomy so common in a christian
> nation, or so notoriously and frequently com-
> mitted, as by too palpable evidences it appears
> to be, in and about this city, notwithstanding
> the clear light of the gospel which shines there-
> in, and the great pains taken to reform the
> abominable profaneness that abounds? Is it not
> a wonder the patience of God hath not con-
> sumed us in his wrath, before this time? Was
> ever swearing, blasphemy, whoring, drunken-
> ness, gluttony, self-love, and covetousness, at
> such a height, as at this time here?[61]

Despite the presence of a number of gospel-centred
ministries like that of Keach and various societies
which had been created to bring about moral
reform,[62] homosexuality, profanity, sexual immorality, drunkenness and gluttony were widespread.
And the next three decades saw little improvement.

The moral tone of the nation was set in many ways
by its monarchs and leading politicians. George I
(r.1714–1727) was primarily interested in food, horses
and women. He divorced his wife when he was thirty-
four and thereafter consorted with a series of mistresses.[63] Sir Robert Walpole (1676–1745), prime
minister from 1722 to 1742, lived in undisguised
adultery with his mistress, Maria Skerrett (d.1738),
whom he married after his wife died.[64] As J.H.
Plumb has noted of aristocratic circles in the early

eighteenth century, the women "hardly bothered with the pretence of virtue, and the possession of lovers and mistresses was regarded as a commonplace, a matter for gossip but not reproach."[65] Not surprisingly other segments of society simply followed suit. Pornographic literature, for instance, multiplied almost unchecked. Newspapers advertised such things as the services of gigolos and cures for venereal disease, and one could purchase guidebooks to the numerous brothels in London.[66] It was, as a recent writer has put it well, "an age when atheism was fashionable, sexual morals lax, and drinking and gambling at a pitch of profligacy that has never since been equalled."[67]

The Hanoverian Church of England, due to its moralism and worldliness described above,[68] was basically helpless when it came to dealing with this dire situation. "Morality of itself," as Whitefield once observed, "will never carry us to heaven."[69] Rather, it was the Revival's message of the new birth and justification by faith alone, trumpeted forth by Whitefield throughout his life, that brought positive changes and hope.

Whitefield's thoughts about the new birth are well seen in a letter to Louise Sophie von der Schulenburg (1692–1773), the Countess of Delitz. The Countess was the illegitimate daughter of George I by one of his mistresses, Melusina von der Schulenburg (1667–1743), the Countess of Kendal. The Countess of Delitz was also a friend of Selina Hastings (1707–1791), the Countess of Huntingdon, and she appears to have been converted through Whitefield's ministry at either Selina's London apartment or Chelsea residence. Writing to the Countess of Delitz from Plymouth in February of 1749, Whitefield rejoices in her conversion.

Blessed be the God and Father of our Lord Jesus Christ, who, I trust, hath imparted a saving knowledge of his eternal Son to your Ladyship's heart. Your letter bespeaks the language of a soul which hath tasted that the Lord is gracious, and hath been initiated into the divine life. Welcome, thrice welcome, honoured Madam, into the world of new creatures! O what a scene of happiness lies before you! Your frames, my Lady, like the moon, will wax and wane; but the Lord Jesus, on whose righteousness you solely depend, will, notwithstanding, remain your faithful friend in heaven. Your Ladyship seems to have the right point in view, to get a constant abiding witness and indwelling of the blessed Spirit of God in your heart. This the Redeemer has purchased for you. Of this he has given your Ladyship a taste; this, I am persuaded, he will yet impart so plentifully to your heart, that out of it shall flow rivers of living waters. This Jesus spake of the Spirit, which they that believe on him should receive. As you have, therefore, honoured Madam, received the Lord Jesus, so walk in him even by faith. Lean on your beloved, and you shall go on comfort-

ably through this howling wilderness, till you
arrive at those blissful regions,

Where pain, and sin, and sorrow cease,
And all is calm, and joy, and peace.[70]

The new birth entails a "saving knowledge" of
the Lord Jesus Christ that is far more than simple
factual knowledge. It marries belief in him as the
"eternal Son" of God to trust in him as one's
Redeemer from sin and its punishment. It means
that one's trust for acceptance by God is no longer
focused on one's own moral achievements but upon
what God has done through Christ's spotless life,
propitiatory death and resurrection. As Whitefield
wrote on another occasion to a different correspondent: "I hope you take particular care to beat down
self-righteousness, and exalt the Lord Jesus alone in
your hearts. I find, the only happiness is to lie down
as a poor sinner at the feet of the once crucified, but
now exalted Lamb of God, who died for our sins
and rose again for our justification."[71]

Moreover, the new birth is intimately bound up
with the gift of the Spirit. Those who experience the
new birth are "initiated into the divine life" as the
Spirit comes to dwell in their hearts. This new birth
ultimately comes from God. Only he can graciously
enable a person to look to Christ alone for salvation.[72]
Finally, it is the new birth alone that sets a person on
the road to heaven. In a sermon that he preached
eleven months later on Ephesians 4:24, Whitefield

put this final point more bluntly: "unless you are new creatures, you are in a state of damnation…I tell thee, O man; I tell thee, O woman, whoever thou art, thou art a dead man, thou art a dead woman, nay a damned man, a damned woman, without a new heart."[73]

Understandably Whitefield was critical of the doctrine of baptismal regeneration, prevalent in many quarters of the Church of England and which he referred to more than once as "that Diana of the present age."[74] His earliest printed sermon, *The Nature and Necessity of our Regeneration or New Birth in Christ Jesus* (1737), was ardent and plain in its rejection of this doctrine. It is "beyond all contradiction," he argued, "that comparatively but few of those that are 'born of water,' are 'born of the Spirit' likewise; to use another spiritual way of speaking, many are baptized with water, which were never baptized with the Holy Ghost."[75] Regeneration is not automatically dispensed when water baptism takes place. Rather, a person must experience "an inward change and purity of heart, and cohabitation of his [i.e. Christ's] Holy Spirit."[76] A genuine Christian is one "whose baptism is that of the heart, in the Spirit, and not merely in the water, whose praise is not of man but of God."[77] It is noteworthy that Whitefield was not afraid of turning the substance of this criticism against the Baptist emphasis on believer's baptism. Writing in the summer of 1741 to a Baptist correspondent in Georgia, he urged him:

I hope you will not think all is done, because you have been baptized and received into full

45

communion. I know too many that "make a Christ of their adult baptism," and rest in that, instead of the righteousness of the blessed Jesus. God forbid that you should so learn Christ. O my dear friend, seek after a settlement in our dear Lord, so that you may experience that life which is hid with Christ in God.[78]

Turning to the doctrine of justification, there is probably no better place to view Whitefield's thinking on this subject than his sermon on 1 Corinthians 1:30, *Christ, the Believer's Wisdom, Righteousness, Sanctification and Redemption*.[79] It was written out early in 1741, while Whitefield was on board ship on his way home to England from Georgia. It appears, though, that he had preached it various times in the preceding months on what was his second visit to America. It was eventually published in Edinburgh, in 1742, and subsequently came out in further editions in other cities in England and America.[80]

After emphasizing that the blessing of justification is rooted in God's everlasting love, Whitefield deals with the first thing that is attributed to Christ, "wisdom." True wisdom, he argues, is not "indulging the lust of the flesh," a reference to the open immorality and godlessness of his day. Nor is it found in the acquisitive "adding house to house." Neither is it merely intellectual knowledge, for "learned men are not always wise."[81] Making the same point to students in New England, Whitefield declared: "Learning without piety, will only make you more capable of promoting the kingdom of Satan."[82]

What then is genuine wisdom? Well, first, Whitefield says, and here he quotes an ancient Greek maxim, it is to "know thyself." What do the children of God need to know about themselves? Well, that before their conversion they were darkness, and now, they are light in the Lord (see Ephesians 5:8). They know something of their lost estate. They see that "all their righteousnesses are but as filthy rags; that there is no health in their souls; that they are poor and miserable, blind and naked." And knowing themselves they know their need of a Saviour. This knowledge is basic and foundational to any biblical spirituality.

The type of self-knowledge that Whitefield is advocating also logically leads to the realization of the need for Christ as one's righteousness. Whitefield develops this thought in terms of Christ's active and passive obedience. By the former Christ fulfills the entirety of the law's righteous demands. This righteousness is imputed to the believer so that he or she now legally possesses the righteousness of Christ. "Does sin condemn? Christ's righteousness delivers believers from the guilt of it." By the latter, Christ passively bears the punishment for the elect's sins—he takes legal responsibility for them, so that God the Father blots out the transgressions of believers, "the flaming sword of God's wrath…is now removed."[83] The

47

spiritual importance of this truth Whitefield later laid out in a letter he wrote to a friend in 1746: "Blessed be his [i.e. Christ's] name if He lets you see more & more that in Him and in Him only you have Righteousness & strength. The more you are led to this foundation, the more solid will be your Superstructure of Gospel holiness."[84]

And the means of receiving these precious benefits of Christ's death? Faith alone—believers, Whitefield affirms in his sermon on 1 Corinthians 1:30, are "enabled [by the Father] to lay hold on Christ by faith." Whitefield clearly indicates that faith itself does not save the sinner—only Christ saves. Faith unites the sinner to the Saviour. Thus, faith, though a necessary means to salvation, is not itself the cause or ground of salvation. As Whitefield says, "Christ is *their* Saviour."[85] Little wonder then that Whitefield, employing the text of Romans 8, goes on to underline the fact that such genuine self-knowledge not only provides the foundation for a truly biblical spirituality but also gives that spirituality a tone of triumphant joy: "O believers!…rejoice in the Lord always."[86] Whitefield knew that when the biblical truth of justification is grasped and appropriated, a deep sense of joy and freedom from the burden of sin floods the heart and one's relationship with God is firmly anchored.

Whitefield has a number of ways of describing this reliance on Christ. In one letter he calls Christ "the believer's *hollow square*." This metaphor is drawn from the European battlefields of the eighteenth century, where armies would regularly form massed squares of infantry three or four rows deep for protection and consolidated strength. If a soldier were wounded his comrades would place him in the centre of the square, where he would be much safer than if he were behind a skirmishing line.[87] "If we keep close" in the square that is Christ, Whitefield continues with the thought of the metaphor, "we are impregnable. Here only I find refuge. Garrisoned in this, I can bid defiance to men and devils."[88]

In another letter, he talks of Christ as the believer's "asylum." Christ's "Wounds and precious Blood is a Sure Asylum & Place of Refuge in every Time of Trouble," he told a friend.[89] In yet a third example, he speaks of Christ alone being able to fill the deepest caverns of the human heart: "Happy they who have fled to Jesus Christ for refuge: they have a peace that the world cannot give. O that the pleasure-taking, trifling flatterer knew what it was! He would no longer feel such an empty void, such a dreadful chasm in the heart which nothing but the presence of God can fill."[90]

"Blessed fruits of the Spirit": The priority of gospel holiness[91]

The new birth and justification by faith alone were hallmarks of Whitefield's spirituality, but so also was a concern for personal and social holiness.[92] Yes, Whitefield never flagged in emphasizing that our acceptance with God can never be based on our sanctification, for the believer's sanctification is always incomplete in this life in a practical sense. Sin, to some degree, still indwells him. "Our most holy thoughts," Whitefield wrote to a friend in early 1741, "are tinctured with sin, and want the atonement of the Mediator."[93] But although faith alone saves, saving faith is never alone. It always issues in good works.

In the sermon *Christ, the Believer's Wisdom, Righteousness, Sanctification and Redemption*, Whitefield thus explicitly rejects the error of those practical antinomians who "talk of Christ without, but know nothing of a work of sanctification wrought within." As Whitefield stresses, "it is not going back to a covenant of works, to look into our hearts, and seeing that they are changed and renewed, from thence form a comfortable and well grounded assurance" of salvation. If "we are not holy in heart and life, if we are not sanctified and renewed by the Spirit in our minds, we are self-deceivers, we are only formal hypocrites: for we must not put asunder what God has joined together."[94] In other words, believers cannot be in union with half a Christ. Or as he puts it pithily in the sermon *The Lord our Righteousness*: "if you are justified by the Blood, you are also sanctified by the Spirit of the Lord."[95]

Whitefield was also unsparing in his criticism of doctrinal antinomianism, which on one occasion he succinctly defined as believers looking for "all...Holiness without," that is, outside of themselves.[96] Its error, in Whitefield's mind, was so overemphasizing freedom from the condemnation of the law that the passionate pursuit of godliness in everyday life was downplayed.[97] He could thus describe it as a "great Evil," "a rank weed" sown by Satan.[98] When doctrinal antinomianism actually began to appear among Whitefield's English colleagues and supporters, in particular through the teaching of William Cudworth (c.1717–1763), Whitefield fervently prayed that Jesus might "crush [this] Cockatrice in its bud."[99]

Following the lead of the New Testament Whitefield never implies that Christians must possess inherent holiness to be reckoned saints. However, he rightly assumes that those who have been made saints by faith alone will indeed lead holy lives. "Live near to Christ," he writes to an American correspondent, and "keep up a holy walk with God. …Hunger and thirst daily after the righteousness of Christ. Be content with no degree of sanctification."[100] Writing to the Countess of Huntingdon on the last day of 1755, he told her: "Every day and every hour must we be passing from death to life. Mortification and vivification make up the whole of the divine work in the new-born soul."[101] Or as he put it to a friend in Philadelphia:

> I trust you will never rest till you are possessed of the whole mind which was in Christ Jesus. He is our pattern; and if we have true grace in our hearts, we shall be continually labouring to

copy after our great exemplar. O the life of Jesus! How little of it is to be seen in those that call themselves his followers. Humility, meekness, love, peace, joy, goodness, faith, and the other blessed fruits of the Spirit, whither are they fled? I fear most take up with the shadow, instead of the substance. God forbid that I, or dear Mr. B—, should be of that unhappy number. Dear Sir, there is an unspeakable fulness, unsearchable riches in Christ. Out of him we are to receive grace for grace. Every grace that was in the Redeemer, is to be transcribed and copied into our hearts. This is Christianity; and without this, though we could dispute with the utmost clearness, and talk like angels, of the doctrines of grace, it would profit us nothing.[102]

Whitefield wisely, and in New Testament fashion, sought to keep the medium between two extremes. On the one hand, he did not insist so much upon Christ's imputed righteousness as to exclude the vital importance of the believer having godliness to evidence that he or she belongs to Christ. But nor did he give such priority to the believer's inherent righteousness as to diminish his or her resting in the righteousness of Jesus Christ alone for salvation.

Whitefield's perspective on the issue of holiness, though it captures well New Testament thinking on the subject, brought considerable grief to the evangelist. For he found himself forced to defend it against two of his closest friends, namely, John and

Charles Wesley.[103]

An honest evaluation of the eighteenth-century Evangelical Revival cannot belittle the central role played in it by John Wesley. One thinks, for instance, of his fearless and indefatigable preaching of Christ crucified for sinners year in and year out throughout the length and breadth of Great Britain after his conversion in 1738. Or there is the genius he displayed in preserving the fruit of the revival in small fellowship groups called "classes." Again, one calls to mind his promotion of the matchless hymnody of his brother Charles, whom J.I. Packer has rightly named "the supreme poet of love to Jesus in a revival context."[104] Yet, for all the good that John Wesley did, he was a lightning-rod for controversy. His propagation of evangelical Arminianism, for example, did much to antagonize Whitefield and other key evangelical leaders.[105]

Equally serious an error was his commitment to the doctrine of Christian perfection. In the year before his death, he plainly indicated his conviction that God had raised up the Wesleyan Methodists primarily for the propagation of this doctrine.[106] Yet, no other doctrine involved Wesley in more controversy than this one. It was a key factor in creating a rift between him and Whitefield, it alienated him from many of the younger leaders in the revival, and eventually it even caused a slight division between him and his brother Charles.[107]

Convinced that Scripture taught this doctrine, though, John Wesley was determined to publish it to the world. Yet, unlike his clear presentation of the heart of the gospel, his teaching about perfection is somewhat murky and at times difficult to pin down. He always contended that he was not advocating "sinless perfection."[108] Yet he could talk about the one who experienced this blessing as having "sin...separated from his soul" and having a "full deliverance from sin."[109] Such perfection freed the person from evil thoughts and evil tempers. As he wrote to the Baptist authoress Ann Dutton (1692–1765), this blessing brings freedom from "all faintness, coldness, and unevenness of love, both towards God and our neighbour. And hence from wanderings of heart in duty, and from every motion and affection that is contrary to the law of love." All this sounds very much like sinless perfection despite Wesley's protest, "we do not say that we have no sin *in us*, but that we do not *commit sin*."[110]

It is curious that Wesley himself never claimed to have experienced Christian perfection, or what he sometimes called "the second blessing."[111] But as he preached it, others did, which to his mind was further confirmation of the scriptural truth of the doctrine. George Whitefield mentions in a letter that he wrote a friend in 1741 that he had met one of Wesley's followers who claimed he had not "sinned in thought, word, or deed" for three months. This man affirmed that he was "not only free from the power, but the very in-being of sin" and asserted that it was "impossible for him to sin." In the same letter Whitefield mentions another, a woman, who

John Wesley

[Reprinted from the frontispiece engraving in Richard Watson, *The Life of the Rev. John Wesley, A.M.* (New York: Carlton & Porter, 1857)]

claimed she had been perfect for an entire year during which time she "did not commit any sin." When he asked her if she had any pride, she brazenly answered, "No!"[112] As Gordon Wakefield wisely sums up Wesley's teaching on Christian perfection: it was "confused, divisive, provoked scandals, errors, mania and the very evils of pride, malice and all uncharitableness it was intended to obliterate forever, and rested on an inadequate concept of sin."[113]

It was from Whitefield that significant opposition to this teaching first came. Despite his friendship with John and almost deferential respect for him, Whitefield was not afraid to challenge his erroneous thinking on Christian discipleship. Between 1740 and 1742 he wrote letters to Wesley and preached a number of sermons which opposed his views about Christian perfection with frankness, but also with evident love. Writing on March 26, 1740, from Savannah, Georgia, for instance, he told Wesley that to the best of his knowledge "no sin has dominion" over him, but he went on, "I feel the strugglings of indwelling sin day by day."[114] Yet, despite his evident conflict with Wesley, he did not relish the prospect of disagreeing with him. Will not their disagreement, he said, "in the end destroy brotherly love, and insensibly take from us that cordial union and sweetness of soul, which I pray God may always subsist between us?"[115]

In September, 1740, Whitefield wrote to a Mr. Accourt of London: "Sinless perfection…is unattainable in this life. Shew me a man that could ever justly say, 'I am perfect.' It is enough if we can say so, when we bow down our heads and give up the ghost. Indwelling sin remains till death, even in the regenerate."[116] Scriptural support for this position was found by Whitefield in texts like 1 Kings 8:46 ("there is no man that sinneth not") and James 3:2 ("in many things we offend all"), as well as examples drawn from the lives of King David and the Apostles Peter and Paul.[117]

Two months later, Whitefield told Wesley: "I am yet persuaded you greatly err. You have set a mark you will never arrive at, till you come to glory." The following month found Whitefield wintering at Bethesda in Georgia. From there he published an open letter against Wesley in which he once again dealt plainly with his brother in Christ. On the subject of perfection he confessed that since his conversion he has "not doubted a quarter of an hour of having a saving interest in Jesus Christ." But, he also had to acknowledge "with grief and humble shame…I have fallen into sin often." Such a confession, though, was not unique to him: it was the "universal experience and acknowledgement… among the godly in every age."[118] Whitefield's perspective rests squarely on the testimony of Scripture, an adequate theological analysis of indwelling sin, and the testimony of God's people in the history of the church.

Wesley's teaching carried enormous weight in the century after his death in 1791. It formed the heart and substance of the transatlantic holiness movement of the nineteenth century. And taking the nomenclature that John Fletcher (1729–1785), Wesley's godly lieutenant, used for Christian perfection, namely his description of it as "the baptism of the Holy Spirit," Wesleyan perfectionism prepared the soil for the emergence of Pentecostalism in this century. What would the later history of Evangelicalism have been like if Wesley had listened to Whitefield? We have no way of knowing, of course, for God's sovereignty deemed otherwise. But it strikes this writer that a much more balanced and clearer perspective on this matter was offered by Wesley's close friend and designated successor, the great Yorkshire evangelist William Grimshaw (1708–1763). It was a perspective that was essentially the position of Whitefield. Writing in March of 1760 to Charles Wesley, Grimshaw stated: "My perfection is to see my own Imperfection. My Comfort to feel that I've the World, Flesh, and devil to overcome, thro' the Spirit and Merits of my Dear Saviour. And my Desire and Hope is to love God with all my Heart, Mind, Soul and Strength to the last Gasp of my Life.—This is my Perfection. I know no other, expecting to lay down my Life and my Sword together."[119]

"An insatiable thirst for travelling": Taking the Word over land and sea

In the early years of the revival Whitefield's itinerant, open-air preaching was often paraded as evidence of his "enthusiasm," or fanaticism. Part of Whitefield's response to this criticism was to go back to the example of the Apostle Paul as found in the Book of Acts. "Was he not filled," he asked his opponents, "with a holy restless Impatience and insatiable Thirst of travelling, and undertaking dangerous Voyages for the Conversion of Infidels...?"[120] Here Whitefield lays before us the spiritual passion that spurred his own incessant travelling over land and sea: the longing to see sinners embrace Christ as Lord and Saviour and find their deepest spiritual thirst and hunger satisfied in Christ alone.

Criticism of the wide-ranging nature of his ministry also came from such ardent Evangelicals as Ebenezer Erskine (1680–1754) and his younger brother Ralph (1685–1752), founders of the Secession Church in Scotland.[121] This body of churches had seceded from the national church in the 1730s over the issue of whether or not the people of a congregation had the right to refuse a minister chosen for them by the Presbytery or heritors (i.e. landowners who possessed hereditary rights to property within a parish). The Erskines had invited Whitefield to preach solely in their churches. But Whitefield refused to be pinned down to a few locales and insisted on preaching wherever he was given a pulpit in Scotland.[122] He told the Erskines that he was "more and more determined to go out into the highways and hedges; and that if the Pope himself would lend me his pulpit, I would gladly proclaim the righteousness of Jesus Christ therein."[123]

That Whitefield failed to understand the concern of the Erskines for the reformation of the church is evident in the sad disagreement between them. Yet, his reply well reveals his passion for the salvation of the lost wherever they might be. As he told the Scottish Lord Rae a few days after this discussion with the Erskines, the "full desire" of his soul was to "see the kingdom of God come with power." He was, he went on, "determined to seek after and know nothing else. For besides this, all other things are but dung and dross."[124] Still in Scotland two months later, the same spiritual desire still deeply gripped him. "I want a thousand tongues to set off the Redeemer's praise," he told the Earl of Leven and Melville.[125]

Five years later, although the surrounding scenery is different—he is on his third preaching tour of America—this passion burned as bright as ever. "Oh that I was a flame of pure & holy fire, & had [a] thousand lives to Spend in the dear Redeemers service," he told Joshua Gee (1698–1748), for the "sight of so many perishing Souls every day affects me much, & makes me long to go if possible from Pole to Pole, to proclaim redeeming love."[126] "Had I a thousand souls and bodies," he noted on another occasion, "they should be all itinerants for Jesus Christ."[127] Six years earlier he told a correspondent that because "Jesus hath of late remarkably appeared for me,"

> I ought to lay myself out more and more in going about endeavouring to do good to precious and immortal souls. At present this is my

settled resolution. The Redeemer seems to approve of it; for the fields in the Southern parts are white ready unto harvest, and many seem to have the hearing ear. All next October, God willing, I have devoted to poor North Carolina. It is pleasant hunting in the woods after the lost sheep for whom the Redeemer hath shed his precious blood. May the Lord of the harvest spirit up more to go forth in his strength, to compel poor sinners to come in![128]

Nothing gave Whitefield greater joy than to report to his friends that God was blessing his preaching. "The word runs and is glorified," a line from Paul's second letter to the Thessalonians (2 Thessalonians 3:1), and Jesus' statement to his disciples that the fields were "white already to harvest" (John 4:35) were frequent refrains in his correspondence. Writing from Pennsylvania in May of 1746, Whitefield informed a correspondent in Gloucestershire, England, that Christ "gives me full employ on this side the water, & causes his word to run & be glorified. ...Everywhere the fields are white ready unto harvest. I am just now going to tell lost sinners that there is yet room for them in the side of Jesus."[129] Upon hearing of the marriage of one of his nephews in 1756, Whitefield observed, "Alas, what a changing world do we live in! Blessed be God for an unchangeable Christ! Amidst all, this is my comfort, his word runs and is glorified."[130] Christ "vouchsafes daily (O amazing love) to own my feeble labours," he told a friend in 1757. Then he added: "The word runs and is glorified."[131] Or writing to a fellow minister in Scotland only a couple of years before his death: "In London the word runs and is glorified, and in Edinburgh, I trust, the prospect is promising. The fields are white ready unto harvest."[132]

Another vantage-point from which to view Whitefield's ministry of the Word is to look at some of the conversions that occurred under his preaching. Out of a multitude of conversion accounts from the eighteenth-century revivals, we choose three.[133] First, that of Thomas Olivers (1725–1799), the Welsh Methodist who was later closely associated with the Wesleys and the author of the well-known hymn "The God of Abraham praise."[134] Notorious for his addiction to foul swearing and in his own words "one of the most profligate and abandoned young men living," Olivers went to hear Whitefield preach in Bristol in 1748. The evangelist's text was Zechariah 3:2: "Is not this a brand plucked out of the fire?" When Whitefield began his sermon, Olivers said,

> I was certainly a dreadful enemy to God and to all that is good,… but by the time it was ended I was become a new creature. For, in the first place, I was deeply convinced of the great goodness of God towards me all my life, particularly in that he had given his Son to die for me. I had also a far clearer view of all my sins, particularly my base ingratitude towards him.

These discoveries quite broke my heart, and caused showers of tears to trickle down my cheeks. I was likewise filled with an utter abhorrence of my evil ways, and was much ashamed that ever I had walked in them. And as my heart was thus turned from all evil, so it was powerfully inclined to all that is good. It is not easy to express what strong desires I had for God and his service, and what resolutions I had to seek and serve him in future; in consequence of which I broke off all my evil practices, and forsook all my wicked and foolish companions without delay, and gave myself up to God and his service with my whole heart.

The first Sunday after his conversion Olivers was up early to attend the six a.m. worship service at Bristol Cathedral. During it, he later said, "I felt as I had done with earth, and was praising God! No words can set forth the joy, the rapture, the awe, and reverence I felt."

Another hymnwriter who made a profession of faith as a result of hearing Whitefield preach, was Robert Robinson (1735–1790).[135] When Robinson first went to hear Whitefield preach his motivation in going was an odd one to say the least. On Sunday morning, May 24, 1752, he and some friends were out looking for some amusement when they came across an aged woman who claimed to be a fortune-teller. After they had gotten her thoroughly drunk on what was probably cheap gin, they proceeded to have her tell their fortunes. When it came to Robinson, the woman predicted that he would live to see his children, grandchildren, and even great-grandchildren growing up around him.

Now, what had started as something of a lark was taken quite seriously by Robinson as he made his way home later that day. When he was alone, he thought that if he were indeed to live to such a ripe age, he would probably end up being a burden to his family. There were in those days no such things as social security or welfare. What then could he do? Well, he thought, one way for those who are older to make themselves liked by their grandchildren is to have a good stock of stories to draw upon to entertain them. He thus determined there and then to fill his mind with knowledge and "everything that is rare and wonderful," which, when he was old, would stand him in good stead and cause him, so he reasoned, to "be respected rather than neglected."[136]

As his first acquisition, he decided to experience one of Whitefield's sermons. He went to hear him, though, as he later told the famous preacher, with feelings of pity for "the folly of the preacher" and "the infatuation of the hearers"—those "poor deluded Methodists,"—and of abhorrence for Whitefield's doctrine.[137]

Whitefield was preaching that evening at the Tabernacle, his meeting-house in Moorfields, London. His text was Matthew 3:7, John the Baptist's stern rebuke of the Pharisees and the Sadducees, "O generation of vipers, who hath

warned you to flee from the wrath to come?"
When, according to Robinson,

> Mr. Whitefield described the Sadducean char-
> acter; this did not touch me, I thought myself as
> good a Christian as any man in England. From
> this he went to that of the Pharisees. He
> described their exterior decency, but observed
> that the poison of the viper rankled in their
> hearts. This rather shook me. At length, in the
> course of his sermon, he abruptly broke off;
> paused for a few moments; then burst into a
> flood of tears; lifted up his hands and eyes, and
> exclaimed, 'O my hearers! The wrath's to come,
> the wrath's to come!' These words sunk into my
> heart, like lead in the waters. I wept, and when
> the sermon was ended, retired alone. For days
> and weeks I could think of little else. Those
> awful words would follow me, wherever I went,
> 'The wrath's to come, the wrath's to come!'[138]

For over three years Robinson was haunted by
these words and Whitefield's sermon. He regularly
attended the preaching at the Tabernacle, and
found himself "cut down for sin" and "groaning for
deliverance." Eventually on Tuesday, December 10,
1755, "after having tasted the pains of rebirth,"
Robinson "found full and free forgiveness through
the precious blood of Jesus Christ."[139] About two
and a half years after his profession of faith
Robinson wrote a hymn long treasured by God's

people: "Come, Thou Fount of every blessing." It appears to have been written to commemorate what God did for him when he saved him.

> Come, Thou Fount of every blessing,
> Tune my heart to sing Thy grace;
> Streams of mercy, never ceasing,
> Call for songs of loudest praise.
> Teach me some melodious sonnet,
> Sung by flaming tongues above;
> Praise the mount; I'm fixed upon it,
> Mount of God's unchanging love.[140]

Robinson eventually went on to pastor St. Andrew's Street Baptist Church.

Another Calvinistic Baptist leader who found Christ as a result of hearing Whitefield was John Fawcett, Sr. (1740–1817). Fawcett was fifteen when he first heard the evangelist preach on John 3:14. Fawcett had gone to church regularly, but he had never heard preaching like this before. By this one sermon alone he was given a clear view of "God reconciled" to sinners "through the atonement of a suffering Saviour." Fawcett's "unbelieving fears" were dispelled, and he was filled with "joy unspeakable and full of glory." For the rest of his life Fawcett kept a portrait of Whitefield in his study and the very mention of his name would prompt "grateful remembrance."[141]

It was important, though, for Whitefield that it was God and Jesus Christ, the ones about whom the Word chiefly spoke, that were glorified and not he himself, the preacher of the Word. A Christ-centredness permeates his correspondence. "What unsearchable riches are there in Jesus [Christ]," he told Jonathan Thompson in the summer of 1746. "What treasures of light & love are hid in Him! May this find you gazing at & admiring them, & by a living faith drawing them down into your soul."[142] Writing around the same time to John Redman (1722–1808), an American who was studying at Guy's Hospital in London and who later became a renowned physician in Philadelphia, he expresses a similar desire. He hoped that his letter found Redman

> admiring the love & beauty of the Great and everblessed[sic] Physician of souls. Blessed be God that I hear you have His interest yet at heart. Look up to Him, my Dear Man, & you shall be kept unspotted from the world. London is a dangerous place. But Jesus is able to deliver you, & make you more than Conqueror over all temptations. May He carry you as a Witness of the power of his resurrection by Land & by sea, & after death give you an Eternal & exceeding weight of glory![143]

The following year he was moved to exclaim in a letter he wrote while in New York:

> Christ is a good Master: he is worthy of all our time, and of everything that we possess. Is not one heart too little for him? And yet he requires

no more. Amazing love! I am lost when I think of it. I can only say, Lord, I adore and worship![144]

His ideal in this regard is found in some lines he wrote to William Pepperell (1696–1759), the commander of the New England militia that captured the fortress of Louisbourg in 1745: "Glory be to our God for what He has done for you & by you, & above all, for enabling you like a pure Crystall [*sic*] to transmitt [*sic*] all the honour He has been pleased to pour upon you, back again to the source from whence it first sprang."[145]

In his correspondence, though, he frequently admitted to wrestling with pride and indwelling sin. "It is difficult," he observed early on in his ministry, "to go through the fiery trial of popularity and applause untainted."[146] This observation came from bitter experience. "I am a proud, imperious, sinful worm," he wrote to Gabriel Harris in 1737.[147] Four years later, we find the same self-evaluation: "I am a poor unworthy sinner, and yet, (O sovereign grace!) the Lord works by me day by day."[148] In 1755 he cried out in one letter,

> O this self-love, this self-will! It is the devil of devils. Lord Jesus, may thy blessed Spirit purge it out of all our hearts! But O how must the divine Paraclete sit as a refiner's fire upon the heart, in order to bring this about! Few choose such fiery purgations, and therefore so few make the progress that might justly be expected

of them in the divine life. Make me, O God, willing to be made, willing to be, to do, or suffer what thou pleasest, and then—what then?—this foolish fluttering heart will sweetly be moulded into the divine image.[149]

In the year this text was written Protestant Britain was on the brink of war with Catholic France—a war that would last until 1763 and would become known as the Seven Years' War—and there was widespread fear of Roman Catholic domination if this war should be lost. Whitefield's main concerns, however, were elsewhere. He could pray for a British victory,[150] but he was convinced that the believer's chief danger and fiercest warfare was with indwelling sin. "O that this time of outward danger," he wrote towards the end of autumn, 1755, "may be sanctified to the exciting of greater zeal against our inward spiritual enemies! For after all, the man of sin in our own hearts, is the greatest foe the real Christian hath to fear."[151]

Despite the intensity of this inner struggle, however, Whitefield could sincerely declare: "Let my name be forgotten, let me be trodden under the feet of all men, if Jesus may thereby be glorified."[152] Nor did this sense of his own sinfulness keep Whitefield silent. In fact, it had the opposite effect. As he told a friend in 1742:

It is good to see ourselves poor, and exceeding vile; but if that sight and feeling prevent our looking up to, and exerting ourselves for our dear Saviour, it becomes criminal, and robs the soul of much comfort. I can speak this by dear-bought experience. How often have I been kept from speaking and acting for God, by a sight of my own unworthiness; but now I see that the more unworthy I am, the more fit to work for Jesus, because he will get much glory in working by such mean instruments; and the more he has forgiven me, the more I ought to love and serve him. Fired with a sense of his unspeakable loving-kindness, I dare to go out and tell poor sinners that a lamb was slain for them; and that he will have mercy on sinners as such, of whom indeed I am chief.[153]

Finally, it should be noted that Whitefield's deep devotion to the person of Jesus Christ stood in vivid contrast to the view of God promoted, consciously or unconsciously, by the moralistic preaching in many quarters of the Anglican church of his day. Although the latter liked to dwell on the universal benevolence of God, lack of involvement with men and women in the hurly-burly of history made it seem distant and very impersonal.

Laying "the soul lower at the foot of Jesus": A Calvinistic spirituality

It is not infrequently asserted that Whitefield did

not have a truly lucid understanding of Calvinism as a body of divinity.[154] As we have seen, he was an evangelist extraordinaire, an itinerant preacher of the Word first and foremost. He certainly never had the time to write out his own systematic treatise on Calvinism. Yet, he was well grounded in the essentials of this theological perspective, as a close reading of both his letters and his sermons reveals. As John Lewis Gilmore has noted of both his sermons and letters, Whitefield was well able to "give a restatement of the classic doctrines of the Reformation in the simplest, most salient language, indicating a digestion of the great doctrines, thoroughly integrated into his thought processes."[155]

Very early in his ministry he identified himself as an heir of the theology of the Reformers and the Puritans. Theirs was a theology that revelled in what Iain Murray has called "the great related chain of truths revealed in the New Testament—the Father's electing love, Christ's substitutionary death on behalf of those whom the Father had given him, and the Spirit's infallible work in bringing to salvation those for whom it was appointed."[156] Writing, for instance, from Philadelphia in 1739 during his first American tour, Whitefield declared:

> Oh the excellency of the doctrine of election, and of the saints' final perseverance, to those who are truly sealed by the Spirit of promise! I am persuaded, till a man comes to believe and feel these important truths, he cannot come out

of himself; but when convicted of these, and assured of the application of them to his own heart, he then walks by faith indeed, not in himself, but in the Son of God, who died and gave himself for him. Love, not fear, constrains him to obedience.[157]

The same day he wrote to another correspondent that "election, free grace, free justification without any regard to works foreseen" are "the truths of God" that "agree with the written word, and the experiences of all the saints in all ages."[158] During his ministry he freely admitted that his theological convictions were "Calvinistical principles"[159] and argued that "the great Doctrines of the Reformation" were what those involved in the Evangelical Revival chiefly sought to propagate.[160] He hoped that he would adhere to "the doctrines of grace" as found in the Anglican *Thirty-nine Articles* and the *Westminster Confession of Faith* all of his life,[161] openly defended those whom he called "the good old Puritans and free-grace Dissenters,"[162] and was convinced that "useful puritanical books" were vital reading for theological students.[163] Whitefield was convinced that if it had not been for the Puritans and those whom he calls "their successors, the free-grace Dissenters," England would have become utterly destitute of vital Christianity and so "void of any spiritual aid in spiritual distresses."[164]

Illustrative of his love of Puritan literature is the following passage, a recommendation of the works of the Puritan evangelist John Bunyan (1628–1688), written towards the end of his life.

> Ministers never write or preach so well as under the cross: the Spirit of Christ and of glory then rests upon them. It was this, no doubt, that made the Puritans of the last century such burning and shining lights. When cast out by the black Bartholomew act and driven from their respective charges to preach in barns and fields, in the highways and hedges, they in an especial manner wrote and preached as men having authority. Though dead, by their writings, they yet speak; a peculiar unction attends them to this very hour; and for these thirty years past I have remarked, that the more true and vital religion hath revived, either at home or abroad, the more the good old Puritanical writings, or authors of a like stamp, who lived and died in the communion of the Church of England, have been called for.[165]

The final sentence in this text is particularly noteworthy, for it draws an explicit link between the Puritans and the Evangelical Revival of Whitefield's own day.[166] Moreover, this recommendation is rooted, as Whitefield notes, in thirty years of appreciative reading of the works of the Puritans.

Like his Puritan predecessors Whitefield valued the written word.[167] And despite the busyness of his life, he found time to read and digest not only Bunyan's writings, but also such Puritan works as

Human Nature in Its Four-fold State by Thomas Boston (1677–1732),[168] Thomas Goodwin's commentary on various passages from Paul's letter to the Ephesians,[169] *The Christian in Complete Armour* by William Gurnall (1617–1679),[170] the annotations on the Scriptures by Samuel Clarke (1626–1701),[171] and some of the works of John Owen (1616–1683).[172] He also read and warmly recommended other Puritan divines, men like John Flavel (*c.*1630–1691),[173] John Howe (1630–1706),[174] Solomon Stoddard (1643–1729),[175] Thomas Halyburton (1674–1712),[176] and was familiar with the life of Philip Henry (1631–1696).[177]

A regular companion from the very beginning of his ministry to its end was Matthew Henry's *Exposition of the Old and New Testament*, a work that "draws on a century of Puritan theology, Bible study and homiletics."[178] Henry, he said, was his "favourite commentator."[179] David Crump, in a fine study of eleven of Whitefield's sermons, notes the way in which Puritanism, "not only in its theology but also in its method of evangelism," shaped Whitefield's preaching. And he suggests that a reading of evangelistic literature by Puritan preachers like Jospeh Alleine (1634–1668) and Richard Baxter (1615–1691) "will quickly show the influences which had molded Whitefield's evangelistic method."[180] Martyn Lloyd-Jones (1899–1981) thus puts it well when he succinctly states that Whitefield "lived in the Puritans and their writings."[181]

There is little doubt that, in part, Whitefield

learned his Calvinism from his reading of the Puritans.[182] But his Calvinism also came to him through a close reading of the Word of God. As he once declared publicly, Calvinism is "Scriptural truth."[183] Thus, he was confident that his friend James Hervey (1714–1758) could read Paul's letters to the Romans and Galatians and find there plainly written the doctrines of justification by faith alone and the imputation of Christ's righteousness to the ungodly.[184]

Morover, the doctrines of grace ran true to Christian experience.[185] Whitefield knew from his own experience and that of countless others he counselled that unless God sovereignly intervenes in a person's life, that person will never willingly leave the thralldom of sin and its tawdry pleasures for the heart-ravishing joys of knowing God in Christ. Man has "a free will to go to hell, but none to go to heaven, till God worketh in him to will and to do after his good pleasure."[186] Then it is only the sovereign work of God through the Spirit of Christ that can give the believer spiritual victory over indwelling sin and the attacks of the devil. As he said in an early letter:

> The doctrines of our election, and free justifi-
> cation in Christ Jesus, are daily more and more
> pressed upon my heart. They fill my soul with
> a holy fire, and afford me great confidence in
> God my Saviour. Surely I am safe, because put
> into his almighty arms. Though I may fall, yet

I shall not utterly be cast away. The Spirit of the Lord Jesus will hold, and uphold me.[187]

Biblical truth brings "new Love" to Christ and "lays the soul lower at the foot of Jesus."[188] The truth of Calvinist doctrine was found in the fact that it did this very thing the best. Writing from Philadelphia on his first visit to the city in 1739, Whitefield observed that it was "the doctrines of the Reformation" that did the most to "debase man and exalt the Lord Jesus. …All others leave freewill in man, and make him, in part at least, a Saviour to himself."[189] When the Connecticut carpenter Nathan Cole (1711–1783) heard Whitefield preach on what was for Cole an unforgettable day— October 23, 1740—he came under deep conviction of his sinfulness as he heard Whitefield outline the spiritual implications of some aspects of Calvinistic truth. "My old foundation was broken up, and I saw that my righteousness would not save me," Cole later wrote. "I was convinced," he continued, "of the doctrine of Election: and went right to quarrelling with God about it; because all that I could do would not save me; and he had decreed from Eternity who should be saved and who not."[190] After two years of spiritual turmoil Cole experienced the new birth and could cry out Whitefield-like: "I thought I could die a thousand deaths for Christ, I thought I could have been trodden under foot of man, be mocked or any thing for Christ—Glory be to God."[191]

Little wonder then that we find Whitefield's

correspondence peppered with such doxological exclamations as "O free grace! Sovereign, electing, distinguishing love!"[192] Reformed theology was utterly central not only to Whitefield's personal experience and his preaching, but also to his understanding of revival and biblical spirituality.[193]

Conclusion

This introduction, lengthy as it is, has not touched upon certain aspects of Whitefield's piety—his high estimation of the Lord's Supper, for instance.[194] Hopefully enough has been provided, though, to verify J.I. Packer's observation that to drink deeply from the well of Whitefield's spirituality is "one of life's richest blessings."[195] It is hoped that this felicity will be further increased as the reader keeps company with Whitefield and his great God in the pages that follow.

Chronology

1714
December 16—Born in the Bell Inn, Gloucester

1732
Matriculates at Pembroke College, Oxford

1735
Spring—Whitefield is converted

1736
June 20—Ordained at Gloucester
June 27—Preaches first sermon,
St. Mary de Crypt, Gloucester

1738
February–May—First voyage to America
May–September—Ministry in the
southern colonies
September–December—Voyage home to England

1739
January 14—Ordained priest in the
Church of England
February 17—Begins open-air preaching
August–October—Second voyage to America

1740
September 24—Visits Harvard
October 17—Visits Jonathan Edwards at
Northampton, Massachusetts

1741
January–March—Voyage back to England
July 24—Embarks at Gravesend for Scotland
November 14—Marries Elizabeth James in
Abergavenny

1742
July—Present at the revival at Cambuslang,
Scotland

1743
October 4—His son, John Whitefield, is born

1744
February 8—Buries his infant son
June 26—Is attacked and almost murdered in
Plymouth
August–October—Third voyage to America

1744-1748
Ministry in America

1748
March—Leaves America for England
March 15—Reaches the Bermudas and begins a
stay of about two months

June–July—Voyage from the Bermudas to England
September 14—Arrives at Edinburgh for
third visit to Scotland

1751
May—Visit to Ireland
July—Arrives at Edinburgh for his fifth
visit to Scotland
August–November—Fourth voyage to America

1752
April–May—Return voyage to England

1754-1755
Fifth preaching tour in America

1757
June–July—Visit to Ireland, where he is physically
attacked in Dublin in early July

1763
June 4—Embarks from Greenock bound for
sixth preaching tour in America

1768
June 15—Is in Edinburgh for his last visit
August 9—Death of Elizabeth Whitefield, his wife

1769
September—Leaves England for
final voyage to America

1770
September 30—Dies at Newburyport,
Massachusetts

1

To Gabriel Harris [1]

Bristol, September 5, 1735

Dear Sir,

How welcome is a line from a faithful friend?—
even as welcome as a shower of rain in a droughty
season. But here's the misfortune, the very kind-
nesses of friends may be cruelty. Commendations,
or even the hinting at them, are poison to a mind
addicted to pride. A nail never sinks deeper than
when dipt in oil. A friend's words may be softer than
butter, and notwithstanding be very swords. Pray
for me, dear Sir, and heal the wounds you have
made. To God alone give glory. To sinners nothing
belongs, but shame and confusion....

P.S. If Mr. Pauncefort's petitions run after this manner for me, I should be thankful: "That God would
finish the good work he has begun in me, that I may
never seek nor be fond of worldly preferment, but
employ every mite of those talents it shall please
God to entrust me with, to his glory and the
church's good, and likewise, that the endeavours of
my friends to revive true religion in the world, may

meet with proper success."[2]

[1] *The Works of the Reverend George Whitefield, M.A.* (London: Edward and Charles Dilly, 1771), I, 10–11. This was either Gabriel Harris, Sr. or his son of the same name. The latter was a boyhood friend. The former was the leading bookseller in the city of Gloucester. See [S.M. Houghton], "Notes" in *Letters of George Whitefield For the Period 1734–1742* (Edinburgh: The Banner of Truth Trust, 1976), 519.

[2] This prayer and Whitefield's admonition to Harris to give the glory to "God alone" are early evidence of Whitefield's Calvinistic piety.

2

To Gabriel Harris [1]

Oxford, April 22, 1736

Dear Mr. H.

[T]his solemn season naturally leads me to say a word or two on a more important subject, the death and passion of our blessed Lord and Saviour. If I mistake not, you commemorate it tomorrow at Crypt.[2] And blessed be God, I do at Christ Church.[3] And oh that we may commemorate it as we ought, that we may fix our thoughts intensely on that great exemplar and all atoning blood, that we may grow in love with his meekness and patience and endeavour daily to be conformed to his most blessed image. Surely we cannot grow angry at trifles, when the Son of God endured such bitter usage, without the least murmur or complaint. Surely, we cannot repine at any dispensations of Providence, tho' ever so severe, when we consider how it pleased God to bruise our Saviour and lay upon him the iniquities of us all.[4] Whatever befalls us is but the due reward of our crimes, but this Redeemer had done nothing amiss; he was killed for our iniquities. I could run through every part of

285

our Lord's sufferings, and show how necessary it is that we should sympathize with him in every particular. But as it now grows late, and I want a little time to prepare for tomorrow's solemnity, you'll excuse me if I now only paraphrase a little on the prayer of the thief on the cross.[4] Lord remember us and pray for us. Lord remember us and rule us. Lord remember us and prepare a place for us. Lord remember us in the hour of death and in the day of judgement.

[1] *Works*, I, 14–15.
[2] St. Mary de Crypt Church, a parish church in Gloucester.
[3] One of the Oxford colleges. It is situated on St. Aldates Street.
[4] Isaiah 53.

3

To Gabriel Harris [1]

Gloucester, June 30, 1736

My Dear Friend,

Glory! glory! glory! be ascribed to an almighty triune God. Last Sunday in the afternoon, I preached my first sermon in the church of St. Mary de Crypt,[2] where I was baptized and also first received the sacrament of the Lord's Supper. Curiosity, as you may easily guess, drew a large congregation together upon the occasion. The sight at first a little awed me. But I was comforted with a heart-felt sense of the divine presence, and soon found the unspeakable advantage of having been accustomed to public speaking when a boy at school and of exhorting and teaching the prisoners and poor people at their private houses whilst at the university. By these means I was kept from being daunted over much. As I proceeded, I perceived the fire kindled, till at last, though so young and amidst a crowd of those who knew me in my infant childish days, I trust, I was enabled to speak with some degree of gospel authority. Some few mocked, but most for the present seemed struck. And I have since heard that a complaint had been made to the bishop that I drove fifteen mad the first sermon. The worthy prelate, as I am informed, wished that the madness might not be forgotten before next Sunday. Before then, I hope, my sermon upon he that is in Christ is a new creature will be completed.[3] Blessed be God, I now find freedom in writing. Glorious Jesus,

> Unloose my stamm'ring tongue to tell
> Thy love immense, unsearchable.[4]

[1] *Works*, I, 18–19.

[2] This first sermon was on Ecclesiastes 4:9–12. See Arnold Dallimore, *George Whitefield: The Life and Times of the Great Evangelist of the Eighteenth-Century Revival* (1970 ed.; repr. Westchester, Illinois: Cornerstone Books, 1979), I, 96–97. It can be found in George Whitefield, *Sermons on Important Subjects* (London: Thomas Tegg, 1833), 107–118.

[3] 2 Corinthians 5:17. The sermon that Whitefield is referring to is *On Regeneration* (*Sermons on Important Subjects*, 543–552).

[4] This quote is from a German hymn translated by John Wesley and which begins thus: "I thirst, Thou wounded Lamb of God." [Houghton], "Notes," 520–521.

4

To Mrs. Harris[1]

Oxford, July 7, 1736

Dear Mrs. H.

Good God! the very idea of what we are to be in glory, transports me while I am writing. There, there, Mrs. H. we shall see the blessed Jesus, whom our souls have so eagerly thirsted after in this life, surrounded with glory, and attended with myriads of his holy angels, who will rejoice at our safe arrival to their happy mansions, and with repeated echoes welcome us to heaven. There, there, we shall not only see, but live with him and enjoy him too, not for a day, a month, a year, an age, but to all eternity. And who can tell the pleasure, comfort, peace, joy, delight, and transport, a glorified saint will feel in the possession of his wished-for, longed-for, ever-adorable, ever-gracious, blessed, beloved, triune God, and that for ever? Surely the happiness will be so great, that eye hath not seen, nor ear heard, neither can the heart of man conceive the thousandth part thereof.[2] And yet, great as it is, I not only wish, but have good hope through Christ, that not only you and Mr. H. but all my Christian friends, and even I myself through grace, shall one day be partakers of it.

1 *Works*, I, 20.
2 1 Corinthians 2:9.

5

To Mrs. Harris[1]

London, December 23, 1737

Dear Mrs. H.

I beseech you Mrs. H. by the mercies of God to pray that the goodness of God may make me humble. As yet the divine strength has been magnified in my weakness. Many have opposed, but in vain. God's power conquers all. I am now going as Abraham did, not knowing whither I go; but I commit myself to the guidance of God's good providence and Spirit. He that has and doth, will deliver me out of all my troubles. I only wish, I could debase myself low enough that I might be more fitted for the high and lofty one who inhabiteth eternity to work by. I am a proud, imperious, sinful worm; but God, I hope, in time, will conform me to the image of his dear Son. He has begun (for ever adored be his free grace), and I trust, he will finish his good work in me.[2]

---

[1] *Works*, I, 32.
[2] See Philippians 1:6.

Whitefield sailing for Georgia

[Reprinted from John Gillies, *Memoirs of Rev. George Whitefield* (New Haven: Horace Mansfield, 1834), facing p.25]

6

To Daniel Abbot[1]

Margret [Margate],
January 9, 1738,
Near 11 at night.

Dear Sir,

Hither the good providence of God has safely brought us. Our ship cast anchor near this town and my dear fellow-traveller and I came ashore to our great comfort to buy some things we wanted. We have been most courteously entertained by the curate of the place. The winds and storms are blustering about our ears and teaching us lessons of obedience as fast as they can. God give us grace to learn them....Oh, dear sir, who would but leave his furied-tattered nets to follow Jesus Christ? Who would but follow the Lamb wherever he shall be pleased to lead him? Pray, dear Mr. Abbot, that I may always do so and then I am sure God will never leave nor forsake me.

You see, dear sir, I have answered your kind letter much sooner than expected to express how sincerely I value your friendship though you differ from me in some outward forms of worship. Indeed, sir, I hope the favours I have received from you and other of your Christian brethren will never go out of my mind, but I shall often plead them as I have done already at the Throne of Grace. I would willingly be of that catholic spirit as to love the image of my divine Master wherever I see it, though, as I told Madam Cook, I should think it a sin in me to dissent from the established church. Yet, I am far from thinking God's grace is confined to any set of men whatsoever. No, I know the partition wall is broken down[2] and that Jesus Christ came to redeem a people out of all nation[s] and languages, and therefore his benefits are not to be confined to this or that particular set of professors. I only wish I may have grace given me to preach the truth as it is in Jesus and then, come what will, I hope I shall (as I do, blessed be God!) rejoice. You know, sir, what a design I am going upon and what a stripling I am for so great a work, but I go forth as David against Goliath in the name of the Lord of Hosts,[3] and I doubt not but he, that has and does, will still deliver unto the end. God give me a deep humility, a well-guided zeal, a burning love, and a single eye, and let men or devils do their worst.

[1] From Graham C.G. Thomas, "George Whitefield and Friends: The Correspondence of Some Early Methodists," *The National Library of Wales Journal*, 26 (1990), 369–370. Used by permission. This letter was written *en route* to America. Whitefield was on board the *Whitaker*, one of three ships that was transporting soldiers to Georgia for the pro-

tection of that colony from the Spanish. Whitefield was to act as chaplain for the duration of the voyage. He had gone on board the ship on December 30, 1737. However, due to contrary winds and storms, the *Whitaker* did not sail from England until February 2, 1738.

2 See Ephesians 2:14.

3 See 1 Samuel 17:45.

Whitefield preaching to soldiers

[Reprinted from John Gillies, *Memoirs of Rev. George Whitefield* (New Haven: Horace Mansfield, 1834), facing p.105]

7

To Mr. — [1]

Gibraltar, February 25, 1738

Dear Mr. —

Any one that knows Gibraltar would be apt to say, Can any good come out from thence? Yes, I assure you, there may; for there are some that are not ashamed of the gospel of Christ. About six o'clock this morning I went to the church, where was assembled a number of decent soldiers praying and singing psalms to Christ as God. They meet constantly three times a day, and I intend, God willing, henceforward to meet them. For my delight is in the saints who are in the earth, and those that excel in virtue.[2] I have talked with some of them, and blessed be God, can find the marks of the new birth in them. They pray without ceasing, have overcome the world, hate sin, love their enemies and one another. They glory in the cross of Christ, and rejoice that they are accounted worthy to suffer shame for the sake of Christ. O, who would but travel to see how the Spirit of God is moving on the faces of poor sinners' souls up and down the world! God, I find, has a people everywhere; Christ has a flock, though but a little flock, in all places.—God be praised, that we are of this flock, and that it will be our Father's good pleasure to give us the kingdom![3]—Gibraltar is blessed with a governor, who hath not absented himself from public worship, unless when he was sick, for these seven years, and yet is very moderate towards the Dissenters.[4] Both conformists and nonconformists perform public worship, though at different times of the day, in the same place. They also have a religious society. The good Lord prosper this work of their hands upon them. Whenever we go away, may we leave a blessing behind us. He is a prayer-hearing God.

[1] *Works*, I, 38.

[2] See Psalm 16:3.

[3] Luke 12:32.

[4] In the eighteenth century the Dissenters would include the English Presbyterians, Congregationalists, Baptists and Quakers. They were also known as Nonconformists. The governor was Joseph Sabine (d.1739), a soldier of about 70 years of age. [Houghton], "Notes," 522.

8

To the Inhabitants of Savannah[1]

From on board the Mary
October 2, 1738

My good Friends,

As God has been pleased to place you more especially under my care, so whether absent or present, I
think it my duty to contribute my utmost endeavours towards promoting the salvation of your precious and immortal souls. For this end, and this only,
God is my judge, came I amongst you; for this end
am I now parted from you for a season; and for this
end do I send you this general epistle. I love, I pray
for, therefore do I write to you all without exception.
But what shall I write to you about? Why, of our
common salvation, of that one thing needful, of that
new birth in Christ Jesus, that ineffable change
which must pass upon our hearts, before we can see
God, and of which you have heard me discourse so
often. Let this, this, my dear friends, be the end of
all your actions. Have this continually in view and
you will never do amiss. The author of this blessed
change is the Holy Ghost, the third person in the
ever-blessed Trinity. The Father made, the Son

redeemed, and the Holy Spirit is to sanctify, and so apply Christ's redemption to our hearts. The means to attain this Holy Spirit, you know and the way you know: Self-denial, and the way of the Cross. "If any man will come after me (says Jesus Christ) let him deny himself, and take up his cross daily, and follow me."[2] And, I cannot but think it a particular blessing, which you enjoy above others; because you are in a new colony, where daily crosses must necessarily fall in your way. O then, I beseech you by the mercies of God in Christ Jesus, make a virtue of necessity, and take up your daily crosses with resignation and thanksgiving.

Another means to attain the Holy Spirit is public worship, for Christ has promised, "where two or three are gathered together in his name, there will he, by his Spirit, be in the midst of them."[3] For your zeal in this particular, I have often blessed God within myself, and made mention of it to others. O continue like-minded, and as in my presence, so in my absence, do not forsake the assembling of yourselves together in the house of God,[4] for there you will have the scriptures read, though not expounded and the Holy Spirit, if you apply to him, will open your understandings, and guide you into all truth.[5]

Many other means there are of attaining the Holy Ghost such as, reading the scriptures, secret prayer, self-examination, and receiving the blessed Sacrament, all which I would insist on, could they be comprised in a letter. But this must be deferred till I see you in person, and am qualified to administer unto you the sacred symbols of Christ's blessed body and blood. In the meanwhile, think not that I shall forget you in my prayers; no, I remember my promise, and whilst the winds and storms are blowing over me, I make supplication to God on your behalf. Though absent in body, I am present in spirit, and joy in hopes of hearing your zeal for the Lord. Remember, my dear friends, that for the space of near four months, I ceased not, day and night, warning every one of you to repent and turn to God, and bring forth fruits meet for repentance.[6] Repent you therefore, and walk in all things as becometh the gospel of our Lord Jesus Christ, and then, and then only, shall your sins be blotted out.

Finally, my brethren, be all of one mind. Let there be no divisions among you; for a kingdom divided against itself cannot stand. Be over careful for nothing, but in every thing, with supplications and thanksgiving make your wants known unto God. Speak not evil one of another, brethren, but live at peace among yourselves; and the God of peace shall in all things direct and rule your hearts.[7] Brethren, pray for us, that God would prosper the works of his hands upon me, and restore me to you as soon as possible. In about eight months, God willing, I hope to see you; in the mean while, you shall not be forgotten by your affectionate, though unworthy minister in Christ Jesus.

1 *Works*, III, 428–430. The discussion in this letter of the "means...of attaining the Holy Ghost" appears to be what today would be called "The ways of experiencing the fullness of the Spirit."

2 Luke 9:23.

3 Matthew 18:20.

4 Hebrews 10:25.

5 John 16:13.

6 See Acts 26:20.

7 See Colossians 3:15.

9

Tullow Bridge, November 20, 1738

Dear Sir,

Though I know you not by name, yet as you were so kind as to come and fetch me to your house, and providence called me so soon away; I think a line will not be unacceptable. But what shall I say, dear sir? Why I thank you with all my soul, for your great kindness, and heartily beseech God it may not lose its reward. But dear sir, give me leave to chide you, for you and many others think more highly of me than you ought to think, for alas! I am nothing, have nothing, and can do nothing without God. What although I may, like a polished sepulchre appear a little beautiful without, yet within I am full of pride, self-love and all manner of corruption. However, by the grace of God I am what I am, and if it should please God to make me instrumental to do the least good, not unto me, but unto him, be all the glory....Oh! dear sir, my heart is so full of a sense of the divine goodness, that I could wish that I could persuade all men to love God; for however this or that pleasure or profit may promise, yet God

Plaque commemorating the open-air preaching of
George Whitefield and John Wesley
at Hanham Mount in 1739

alone can procure true happiness to the soul.

Therefore, dear sir, make God the alpha and omega, the beginning and end of all your actions. Study to know him more and more, for the more you know, the more you will love him. Study to know him as he has revealed himself in Christ Jesus, and labour every day to copy after that exemplar. In short, renounce the world in affection, deny yourself, and give your heart to God, and he in return will give you himself.

[1] "Original Letter of the late Rev. George Whitfield [*sic*]," *The Baptist Magazine*, 1 (1809), 266–267.

10

To a minister [1]

Philadelphia
November 10, 1739

Rev. and dear Sir,

Though but little acquainted with you, yet I write this to assure you, what a cordial respect I have for you. The love of God, which I trust, through his free grace, is shed abroad in both our hearts,[2] constrains me to love you in the bowels of Jesus Christ. I remember you in my unworthy prayers, and am persuaded I am not forgotten in yours. No one more needs them, whether considered as a private Christian, or a public minister; thousands are waiting for my halting; and I know so much of the corruption of my own heart, that was God to leave me to myself but one moment, I should with oaths and curses deny my master. As for my final perseverance, I bless God, I have not the least doubt thereof. The gifts and callings of God are without repentance. Whom he loves, I am persuaded, he loves to the end. But then I fear, lest being puffed up with abundance of success, I should provoke the Lord to let me fall into some heinous sin, and thereby give his adversaries reason to rejoice. A public life is attended with innumerable snares; and a sense of my unworthiness and unfitness so weighs me down, that I have often thought it would be best for me to retire. But I know these are all suggestions of the enemy. Why should I distrust omnipotence? Having had a legion of devils cast out of my heart by the power of Christ, why should I not tell what he hath done for my soul, for the encouragement of others. By the help of God, I will speak; and the more Satan bids me to hold my peace, the more earnestly will I proclaim to believing saints, that Jesus the son of David will have mercy on them.[3]

---

1 *Works*, I, 76–77. According to Houghton, this letter "seems to be written to a minister at Wethersfield, about eight miles from Thaxted, where Whitefield had preached on 22 June, 1739" ("Notes," 525).

2 See Romans 5:5.

3 See Luke 18:38.

11

To students [1]

Philadelphia
November 10, 1739

My dear Brethren in Christ,

I heartily pray God, that you may be burning and shining lights in the midst of a crooked and perverse generation.[2] Though you are not of the Church of England, yet if you are persuaded in your own minds of the truth of the way wherein you now walk, I leave it. However, whether Conformists, or Nonconformists, our main concern should be, to be assured that we are called and taught of God; for none but such are fit to minister in holy things. Indeed, my dear brethren, it rejoiced me much to see such dawnings of grace in your souls; only I thought most of you were bowed down too much with a servile fear of man: but as the love of the Creator increases, the fear of the creature will daily decrease in your hearts. Nicodemus, who came at first by night to our Lord, afterwards dared to own him before the whole council in open day. I pray God make you all thus minded. For unless your hearts are free from worldly hopes and worldly

Philip Doddridge

fears, you never will speak boldly, as you ought to speak. The good old Puritans, I believe, never preached better, than when in danger of being taken to prison as soon as they had finished their sermon. And however the Church may be at peace now, yet I am persuaded, unless you go forth with the same temper, you will never preach with the same demonstration of the Spirit, and of power.[3] Study therefore, my brethren, I beseech you by the mercies of God in Christ Jesus, study your hearts as well as books—ask yourselves again and again, whether you would preach for Christ, if you were sure to lay down your lives for so doing? If you fear the displeasure of a man for doing your duty now, assure yourselves you are not yet thus minded. But enough of this, I love to hope well of you all. I trust, as you are enlightened with some degree of knowledge in the mysteries of Godliness, you will henceforth determine not to know anything but Jesus Christ, and him crucified.[4]

---

[1] *Works*, I, 81–82. This letter was written to the students at the Academy of Philip Doddridge (1702–1751) in Northampton, England ([Houghton], "Notes," 525). Doddridge was a leading Congregationalist minister who had deep sympathies with the leaders in the revival. As W.R. Ward puts it: by the 1740s Doddridge "was a Methodist in the sense of an adherent of the movement of revival and reform" [*The Protestant Evangelical Awakening* (Cambridge: Cambridge University Press, 1992), 348]. For Doddridge's sympathy with the revival, see also Alan C. Clifford, "Philip Doddridge and the Oxford Methodists," *Proceedings of the Wesley Historical*

Society, 42 (December 1979), 75–80.

Doddridge himself had first written to Whitefield on December 12, 1738, and enquired as to whether he had any intentions of coming near Northampton, where Doddridge lived. Although the two had never met, Doddridge wrote that he would "gladly undertake a day's journey to meet and confer" with Whitefield, so that he might, as he puts it, "light my lamp by yours and gain that assistance in my way heavenward which a knowledge of you will, I hope, give me." [Letter to George Whitefield, December 12, 1738, in Graham C.G. Thomas, "George Whitefield and Friends: The Correspondence of Some Early Methodists," *The National Library of Wales Journal*, 27 (1992), 65]. It appears that the two men met for the first time on May 23, 1739, when Whitefield preached in the open air to around 3,000 people at Northampton. In his *Journal* Whitefield mentions that prior to his preaching he had been "most courteously received by Dr. Doddridge" [*George Whitefield's Journals* (London: The Banner of Truth Trust, 1960), 273]. The following month Doddridge thanked God in his *Diary* for "adding to me the friendship of some excellent persons, among whom I must mention Mr. Whitefield and Colonel Gardiner" [*The Correspondence and Diary of Philip Doddridge, D.D.*, ed. John Doddridge Humphreys (London: Henry Colburn and Richard Bentley, 1831), V, 401]. Four years later, Doddridge preached for Whitefield at his Tabernacle in London, which caused quite a stir among his fellow Dissenters. Doddridge reciprocated by having Whitefield preach at his church in Northampton in October of that year. For a good study of his life, see Malcolm Deacon, *Philip Doddridge of Northampton 1702–1751* (Northampton: Northamptonshire Libraries, 1980).

2 Philippians 2:15.

3 1 Corinthians 2:4.

4 1 Corinthians 2:2.

12

To John Wesley [1]

Savannah, March 26, 1740

Honoured Sir,

I could now send a particular answer to your last; but, my honoured friend and brother, for once hearken to a child, who is willing to wash your feet. I beseech you by the mercies of God in Christ Jesus our Lord, if you would have my love confirmed towards you, write no more to me about misrepresentations wherein we differ. To the best of my knowledge at present, no sin has dominion over me,[2] yet I feel the strugglings of indwelling sin day by day; I can therefore by no means come into your interpretation of the passage mentioned in the letter, and as explained in your preface to Mr. Halyburton[3]— the doctine of election, and the final perseverance of those that are truly in Christ, I am ten thousand times more convinced of, if possible, than when I saw you last. You think otherwise: why then should we dispute, when there is no probability of convincing? Will it not in the end destroy brotherly love, and insensibly take from us that cordial union and sweetness of soul, which I pray God

Whitefield canoeing to Savannah

may always subsist between us? How glad would the enemies of the Lord be to see us divided? How many would rejoice, should I join and make a party against you? And in one word, how would the cause of our common master every way suffer by our raising disputes about particular points of doctrine? Honoured Sir, let us offer salvation freely to all by the blood of Jesus; and whatever light God has communicated to us, let us freely communicate to others. I have lately read the life of Luther, and think it in no wise to his honour, that the last part of his life was so much taken up in disputing with Zuinglius and others; who in all probability equally loved the Lord Jesus, notwithstanding they might differ from him in other points.[4] Let this, dear Sir, be a caution to us, I hope it will to me; for by the blessing of God, provoke me to it as much as you please, I do not think ever to enter the lists of controversy with you on the points wherein we differ. Only I pray to God, that the more you judge me, the more I may love you, and learn to desire no one's approbation, but that of my Lord and master Jesus Christ....

Oh, dear honoured Sir, I wish you as much success as your own heart can wish. Was you here, I would weep over you with tears of love, and tell you what great things God hath done for my soul, since we parted last. Indeed and indeed, I often and heartily pray for your success in the gospel. May your inward strength and outward sphere increase day by day! May God use you as a choice and singular instrument of promoting his glory on earth, and may I see you crowned with an eternal and exceeding weight of glory in the world to come! This is the hearty desire of, honoured Sir,

Yours most affectionately in Christ Jesus, G.W.

1 *Works*, I, 155–157.
2 See Romans 6:14.
3 Thomas Halyburton (1674–1712), a Scottish divine.
4 This is a reference to the quarrel between Martin Luther (1483–1546) and Huldreich Zwingli (1484–1531) over the nature of Christ's presence in the Lord's Supper.

13

To Howel Harris in Wales [1]

Philadelphia
November 9, 1740

My very dear Brother Harris,

I wrote to you from Boston. Your letter, written near a twelve-month ago, came to my hand this afternoon. My soul is knit to you; we both speak and think the same things. The Lord be with your spirit. Jesus manifests forth his glory daily in these parts. Though I am such a vile, worthless, ungrateful wretch, yet the Lord fills me out of his divine fullness day by day. His word is like a fire, and a hammer;[2] last week I saw many quite struck down. Our Lord is working upon little children. America, ere long, will be famous for Christians. Surely the candlestick will shortly be removed from England. Little did I think, when Mr. E— J— wrote,[3] that I should preach in all the chief places of America: but that is now done; glory be to rich, free, and sovereign grace!

---

[1] *Works*, I, 220. Howel Harris (1714–1773), a schoolmaster by profession, was converted around the same time as Whitefield, Easter 1735. His conversion was the catalyst of the Welsh

Howel Harris

[Reprinted from *Wesley His Own Biographer* (London: C.H. Kelly, 1891), p.130]

Revival. Burdened by the spiritual state of his family, friends and neighbours he began to preach the Gospel in the evenings after he had finished teaching for the day. He tried to survive on two hours of sleep at night, but eventually at the end of 1737 he was issued with an ultimatum: either give up preaching or leave the school. He chose the latter. From then until 1749 he was engaged in itinerant evangelism like Whitefield.

Following a punishing schedule of preaching and exhorting, often without adequate meals and rest, he began to assert aberrant theological views towards the end of this period. He maintained at this period in time, for instance, a modalistic view of the Trinity and claimed to possess the Apostolic gift of prophecy. Not surprisingly, these views caused division within the revival in Wales. From 1751 to 1753 he was a very sick man and was frequently confined to his bed in a deranged state. God was gracious to him, though. After apologizing for his errors, he was once again active in the 1760s.

Shortly before his death, Harris received a letter from one of his firmest supporters, Edmund Jones (1702–1793) of Pontypool, that well puts his career in perspective. "Everywhere, where the gospel is preached," Jones told Harris, "there is no want of people to hear: & you sir, thro the favour of God's providence have been at the bottom of all this, …you have been a great Instrument of Conversion" [cited Geoffrey F. Nuttall, *Howel Harris 1714–1773: The Last Enthusiast* (Cardiff: University of Wales Press, 1965), 57]. On his life and extraordinary ministry, see Hugh J. Hughes, *Life of Howell Harris, The Welsh Reformer* (1892 ed.; repr. Hanley, Stoke-on-Trent: Tentmaker Publications, 1996); Edward Morgan, *The Life and Times of Howell Harris: The First Itinerant Preacher in Wales* (1852 ed.; repr. Denton, Texas: Need of the Times Publishers, 1998). For a more recent study, see Nuttall, *Howel Harris 1714–1773*.

[2] See Jeremiah 23:29.

[3] Houghton suggests that this is probably Edmund Jones, mentioned above in n.1 ("Notes," 537).

14

To Mr. G– C– [1]

On board the Savannah *for Georgia*
December 11, 1740

My Brother George,

Your late letters, especially that which you sent me by way of Charlestown, made me smile. I was glad to find that you had not so far thrown off all outward things, as to resolve not to write to any one; and I thought I knew the frame of your heart, as though I was within you. My dear, dear George C—, I love you tenderly in the bowels of Jesus Christ, and therefore would not have you be deceived. Alas, why do you pervert this text of scripture, "Be still, and know that I am the Lord," as if it was designed to keep a Christian from striving, or meant a stillness of body, or waiting upon God only in silence? [2] The expression is taken out of the 46th Psalm, where God's fury against the heathen is described in the most lively colours; and then lest his people should complain of the severity of his dispensations, God commands them to be *still*, "not to murmur or repine, knowing that he was the Lord, and might do what seemed him good." Thus

Tate and Brady in the translations explain it,[3] and this is the true and genuine meaning of that sentence. It hath no reference to stillness in prayer, or stillness of body.

Dear brother, I speak to you plainly, because I love you. I think I know what it is to wait upon the Lord in silence, and to feel the Spirit of God making intercession for me with groanings which cannot be uttered.[4] Often I have been at such times filled as it were with the fullness of God, and I do now daily carry on a communion with the most high God and the ever-blessed Jesus. But all this I fear is contrary to the false stillness, you and some others seem to have fallen into. I was just in the same case some years ago at Oxford, when I declined writing, reading, and such like exercises, because I would be *still*. The Lord convinced me; I pray he may also convince you of this delusion. Dear George, consider how contrary your maxim is to our Saviour's. You say, "*Be still*." He says, "*Strive*," as in an agony, "Strive that you may enter in at the strait gate."[5] Indeed, my dear man, I pity you, knowing you have but a weak judgement, though a well-meaning heart.

You once thought that you was born again; then, you found it was only an elapse of the Holy Ghost. You used to say, you wished you could believe from experience in the doctrine of election; now, you find as yet no evidence within yourself that you are a real Christian. You take too much refuge, I fear, in the doctrine of universal redemption. It is the finest doctrine in the world to cause a soul to be falsely still, and to say *Peace, Peace*, when there is no peace. You seem to insist upon sinless perfection, and to think a man hath no real salvation till he literally cannot commit sin. From whose experience do you write this? Not from your own, dear George; for I much question, if ever your heart was truly broken or had a saving closure with Christ. You seem to mention Peter Böhler[6] as an instance; but alas, though he has been washed in the blood of the Lamb, so as to be justified from all his sins, yet like me his feet want washing still,[7] and will, till he bows down his head and gives up the ghost. I have conversed with him intimately. Take heed, brother, of having any thing too much in admiration, or of thinking you must necessarily find Christ at such and such a place.

...If God loves you, he will let you see the vanity of your present imaginations, and bring you to see that salvation is not of him that willeth, nor of him that runneth, but of God that sheweth mercy.[8] Dear George, be not given to change; be not too fond of new things. "To the law and to the testimony,"[9] and see what Christ and his apostles have spoken. I speak this out of love, and not in reference to myself. If God blesses another ministry to your soul, I rejoice, yea and will rejoice. But if I see you fall into errors, do not be angry if I tell you the truth. If you are, I will notwithstanding love and pray for you. That errors are crept in among you, I think is too plain: but I suspend my judgment till the spring, when,

God willing, I hope to be in London.

In the meanwhile pray for me, that I may with joy bear to be deserted by those, who once were blessed and awakened by my ministry, and to whom I am a spiritual father, though they may have many instructors. Dear George, may the Lord be with you. He only knows how dear you are to my heart. It is near midnight; but it was much upon my heart to write you this letter. That God may sanctify it to your edification and comfort, it is the hearty prayer of

Your affectionate friend, brother and
servant in Christ,
G.W.

1 *Works*, I, 227–229. The background to this letter is the stillness controversy of the early 1740s. In 1739 a Moravian missionary by the name of Philipp Heinrich Molther (1714–1780) began to teach in London that those who professed faith in Christ should abstain from the means of grace—such things as worship, the reading of the Bible, the Lord's Supper—until all doubts were removed from their minds and hearts. His teaching exercised a great influence among some of the earliest converts of the revival. Among them was the recipient of this letter. Moreover, those who imbibed this teaching often lost the aggressive passion for evangelism. By contrast, Whitefield's spirituality, like that of the Wesleys, was a highly strenuous one in pursuit of both holiness and the salvation of the lost. And in his mind, essential to growth in holiness were the means of grace. On Molther, see C.J. Podmore, "Molther, Philipp Heinrich" in Donald M. Lewis, ed., *The Blackwell Dictionary of Evangelical Biography 1730–1860* (Oxford/Cambridge, Massachusetts: Blackwell Publishers, 1995), II, 780–781. On the stillness

controversy, see especially Clifford W. Towlson, *Moravian and Methodist: Relationships and Influences in the Eighteenth Century* (London: The Epworth Press, 1957), 79–117. For a discussion of the spirituality that Molther's views produced, see John Walsh, "The Cambridge Methodists" in Peter Brooks, ed., *Christian Spirituality: Essays in Honour of Gordon Rupp* (London: SCM Press Ltd., 1975), 263–283.

2 Psalm 46:10.

3 Nahum Tate (1652–1715) and Nicholas Brady (1659–1726) were the authors of the New Version of the Psalms (1696). This work was constantly reprinted throughout the eighteenth century.

4 Romans 8:26.

5 Luke 13:24.

6 Peter Böhler (1712–1775) was a German-speaking Moravian missionary who was instrumental in the conversion of both John and Charles Wesley. According to W.R. Ward, Böhler's life was charactereized by "a quiet humility and a capacity to expound the Gospel to educated and untutored hearers in a variety of languages" ("Böhler, Peter" in Lewis, ed., *Evangelical Biography 1730–1860*, I, 115–116. On Böhler, also see Nehemiah Curnock, ed., *The Journal of the Rev. John Wesley, M.A.* (London: Epworth Press, 1960), I, 436, n.1.

7 An allusion to John 13:6–10, where Jesus washed the feet of his disciples.

8 Romans 9:16.

9 Isaiah 8:20.

Anne Dutton

15

To Mrs. Anne Dutton [1]

On board the Minerva
February 20, 1741

My dear Sister,

My conscience almost reproaches me, that I have not wrote to you often, nor full enough; accept this as an acknowledgement of my fault. I am sorry for it. We are now about a thousand miles off England. I hope this will provoke you to send me a letter immediately after my arrival. I find Luther's observation to be true: "Times of reformation are times of confusion." [2] As yet the churches in America are quiet, but I expect a sifting time ere long. My family in Georgia was once sadly shaken, but now, blessed be God, it is settled, and, I hope, established in the doctrines of grace. Your name is precious among them. I wish you would send them a long letter. Your book on *walking with God* has been blessed to one Mr. Bryan, and others in South-Carolina. [3] It hath also been serviceable to a dear friend now with me, as also to myself.

I cannot well tell you what great things are doing abroad. I have a scene of sufferings lying before me;

I expect shortly to cry out with the spouse, "Look not upon me, because I am black, because the sun hath looked upon me, my mother's children were angry with me."[4] My Lord's command, now, I believe, is, "Take the foxes, the little foxes that spoil the vines; for our vines have tender grapes."[5] Help me by your prayers. It is an ease thus to unbosom one's self to a friend, and an instance of my confidence in you. O, my dear Sister, I am less than the least of all saints, I am the chief of sinners,[6] and yet Jesus loves me, and sheds his love abroad in my heart abundantly by the Holy Ghost.[7]

I have been much afflicted in composing some gospel sermons, which I intend for the press. I have sought the Lord by prayer and fasting, and he assures me, that he will be with me. Whom then should I fear? Hitherto we have had an extraordinary passage, praise the Lord. Herewith I send you a letter from one of the children which God has given me. He will rejoice to receive a line from you. If possible, I hope, tho' you are in the decline of life, to see you face to face before I leave England. I should be glad to hear how you are as to worldly circumstances; if I can help you in any degree, freely command.

Your affectionate friend, brother, and servant,
in Christ,
G.W.

1 *Works*, I, 250–251. Anne Dutton (1692–1765) was a prolific author of spiritual tracts and theological treatises. A Particular (i.e. Calvinistic) Baptist by conviction, she maintained an extensive correspondence with key figures associated with the Evangelical Revival, including Whitefield, Howel Harris, and John Wesley. As is evident from this letter, Whitefield highly regarded her and her writings. Harris apparently told her: "our Lord has entrusted you with a Talent of writing for him" [cited Stephen J. Stein, "A Note On Anne Dutton, Eighteenth-Century Evangelical," *Church History*, 44 (1975), 487–488]. On the other hand, Wesley, of whose views on Christian perfection she was critical, was not so appreciative. For her life, see J.C. Whitebrook, "The Life and Works of Mrs. Anne Dutton," *Transactions of the Baptist Historical Society*, 7, Nos. 3–4 (1921), 129–146; Stein, "Note On Anne Dutton," 485–491; JoAnn Ford Watson, "Anne Dutton: An Eighteenth Century British Evangelical Woman Writer," *Ashland Theological Journal*, 30 (1998), 51–56.

2 Whitefield has in mind the stillness controversy (see pp.124–125, n.1) and the controversy with the Wesleys over the doctrines of grace and Christian perfection (see pp.52–58).

3 The "Mr. Bryan" is either Hugh Bryan or his brother Jonathan, both of whom had been converted under Whitefield's preaching and who were prominent South Carolina plantation owners. The book to which Whitefield is referring is Anne Dutton's *A Discourse upon Walking with God* (London, 1735).

4 Song of Solomon 1:6.

5 Song of Solomon 2:15.

6 Ephesians 3:8; 1 Timothy 1:15.

7 Romans 5:5.

16

To Titus Knight, at London [1]

On board the Minerva
February 20, 1741

My dear Brother Knight,

I find, since my departure, the brethren have fallen into errors. Dear Brother Knight will not be offended, if I say; "He, I fear, is one of them"; for his letter bewrayeth[2] him. My dear Brother, you say, "You have been striving a long, long while, but to very little purpose, etc." By this, I suppose, you have left off the means,[3] and fallen into stillness; expecting now, that Jesus Christ will so work upon your heart, that you shall not feel the least stirring of indwelling corruption in your soul; in short, that you shall be completely perfect. This was pretty near my case about six years ago, and now I see why God suffered me thus to be tempted, "that I might be more capable of succouring my brethren, now they are tempted."

My dear Brother, let us reason together. "You have been striving (you say) a long while, but to very little purpose." And what then? Must you be therefore still, and strive no more? God forbid. No, you are yet to wait at the pool.[4] "Constantly attend on ordinances," and who knows but by-and-by the loving Saviour may pass by and visit your soul. Have you not, in some degree at least, felt his divine power in the use of the means? Why should not that encourage you to expect more in the same way? But you say, "I find all that is of self is sin." And do you expect ever to do anything, or to offer up to God one sacrifice, without a mixture of sin in it? If you do, indeed you are building a spiritual Babel. My dear Brother, even our most holy thoughts are tinctured with sin, and want the atonement of the Mediator; and therefore, if you leave off striving, because "whatever is of self is sin," you must never attempt to do any duty whatsoever again. Your still-ness hath as much a mixture of self in it, as your striving, and if you proceed in this manner, you must become a professed Quietist.[5] Six weeks did Satan keep me under this delusion, but the Lord helped me in the hour of extremity. May he also help my dear Brother Knight!

Another error you seem to be fallen into is "that a man cannot be a Christian, at least that he is a very weak one, so long as he finds corruption stirring in his heart." If I was to urge the seventh [chapter in the letter] to the Romans, you would say, St. Paul only speaks of a man under first awakenings, and not of a converted man. But my dear Brother, did you ever know a man that was not really converted delight in the law of God after the inner man?[6] And yet such a one the Apostle speaks of in the latter part of that chapter. Be not deceived, we are to be holy as Christ is holy; we are to receive grace for grace; every grace that is in the blessed Jesus is to be transplanted into our hearts; we are to be delivered from the power, but not from the indwelling and being of sin in this life.[7] Hereafter, we are to be presented blameless, without spot, or wrinkle, or any such thing. If you labour after any other perfection here, you will labour in vain. St. Paul had attained no other, when he wrote to the Philippians, and to the other churches.[8]

But my dear Brother Knight seems to think, "I did wrong in writing to Mr. H— to know his sentiments upon several texts of scripture, and in sending for several of Calvin's books." And why, my dear Brother, was this wrong? Why you say, "you think it is contrary to St. Paul in his Epistles, when he says, he would not speak other men's words." But St. Paul says no such thing. The place you aim at, I believe, is 2 Cor x. 16, "And not to boast in another man's line of things made ready to our hand." My dear Brother, examine the context, and you will find the Apostle means no more than that he would not enter into other men's labours, as verse 15. He would not preach where churches were already settled, but go where the gospel had not been delivered. This, and this only, is the meaning of the passage, which dear mistaken Mr. Knight has wrongly quoted. My dear Brother, did not St. Paul bid Timothy to give himself to reading?[9] What, if the Holy Spirit is to lead us into all truth,[10] does not the

Holy Spirit make use of, and lead us by the means? Has he not indited the scriptures? Has he not helped holy men to explain those scriptures? And why may I not, in a due subordination to the Holy Spirit, make use of those men's writings? Has not my dear Brother Knight bought sermons? And why then does "He make use of other men's words?" O, my dear brother, you are in the wilderness; God bring you safe out of it.

I suppose because the Dissenters oppose some of your new principles, you term them enemies. But, my dear Brother, though there are many Christless talkers, and hypocritical formalists among the Dissenters, as no doubt there are some such in the purest church under heaven, yet many of them hold and practice the truth as it is in Jesus.

1 *Works*, I, 251–253. Houghton identifies the recipient of this letter as Titus Knight, later a minister in Halifax and who wrote an elegy on Whitefield after learning of his death in 1770 ("Notes," 540).

2 i.e. reveals.

3 i.e. the means of grace.

4 An allusion to John 5:3–4.

5 The Quietists strictly speaking were a circle of seventeenth-century Roman Catholic writers such as Miguel de Molinos (*c*.1640–1697) and Madame Guyon (1648–1717), who promoted the idea that total passivity is the pathway to Christian perfection.

6 Romans 7:22.

7 See also Whitefield's words in a letter written on February 5, 1742: "there is an unspeakable fullness, unsearchable riches in Christ. Out of him we are to receive grace for grace. Every

grace that was in the Redeemer, is to be transcribed and copied into our hearts. This is Christianity; and without this, though we could dispute with the utmost clearness, and talk like angels, of the doctrines of grace, it would profit us nothing" (*Works*, I, 367).

8 Philippians 3:12.

9 1 Timothy 4:13: "give attendance to reading" (KJV). The Greek term for reading, *anagnōsis*, that the Apostle Paul uses in this verse actually refers to the public reading of the Scriptures in a worship context. Whitefield's view of the importance of theological and spiritual reading, however, is not misguided. An anti-intellectual spirit has often bedevilled Evangelicalism and Whitefield did well to oppose it.

10 See John 16:13.

17

To Mr. Howel Harris [1]

Bristol, April 28, 1741

My dear Brother,

Blessed be God for knitting us together in love. May it continue, and increase till consummated in eternity! The Lord Jesus direct you. It is now a trying time with the church. Our Lord is now chiefly wounded in the house of his friends. The Lord keep us both from a party spirit on one hand, and from too much rashness and postiveness on the other. I speak thus, because you seem offended that some affirm, "That there is no such thing as dominion over indwelling sin, nor rest from working for life wholly." Now this is certainly true in one sense. We shall never have such a dominion over indwelling sin, as entirely to be delivered from the stirring of it; and the greatest saint cannot be assured, but some time or other for his humiliation, or punishment for unfaithfulness, God may permit it to break out into some actual breach of his law, and in a gross way too. Let us not be high-minded, but fear.

It is equally true, that we shall not rest wholly from working for life. For whilst there is any part of us unregenerate, that part will be always leading us to the old covenant. Luther often complained of the propensity of his heart this way. If we know ourselves, we shall find it to be so with us; but I suppose you have been tinctured with the doctrine of sinless perfection. No wonder therefore you write thus. May God give you a right judgement in all things, and enable you rightly to divide the word of truth![2]

As for assurance, I cannot but think, all who are truly converted must know that there was a time in which they closed with Christ. But then, as so many have died only with an humble hope, and have been even under doubts and fears, though they could not but be looked upon as Christians, I am less positive than once I was, lest haply I should condemn some of God's dear children. The farther we go in the spiritual life, the more cool and rational shall we be, and yet more truly zealous. I speak this by experience. Dear brother Harris will not be angry with me. I hope, and believe, you pray for me. The Lord Jesus carries me on. Many have been convinced at London. I preach here twice daily, to large congregations, with great power. The Lord, I believe, will yet bring mighty things to pass. I am, dear Howel,

Your most affectionate brother in our Lord Jesus,
G.W.

[1] *Works*, I, 259–260. For the identification of this letter as being written to Harris, see L. Tyerman, *The Life of the Rev. George Whitefield* (New York: Anson D. F. Randolph & Co., 1877), I, 478–479.
[2] 2 Timothy 2:15.

18

To Howel Harris [1]

London, June 6, 1741

My Brother Howel Harris

I do assure you, that my heart is as your heart. I am quite sick of Christless consenters. They talk, and that is all. I (like you) am heartily despised by most of them. I am resolved to open against their lukewarmness, and worldly-mindedness. May God open my mouth wide when I come to *Wales*. Outward enemies are now more quiet. Enemies within the church, carnal professors, and self-righteous Pharisees, most try us. Let us not fear, Jesus Christ will give us the victory over all. God mightily strengthens me. Our congregations are very large and solemn. I never had greater freedom in preaching. God enables me to cast all my care upon him, with a full assurance that he careth for me.

You need not fear my believing any reports to your disadvantage. I love you in the bowels of Jesus Christ. I was not in the least offended, when B— H— wrote me word that "you thought in some things I did not act as a little child." The more open you are with me the better. If nature and pride rise in my heart, I will go to Jesus, abhor myself, and pray for my dear reprovers. All that I can say is, that I desire to be a very little child. All things are possible with Jesus Christ. He is wonderfully kind to me. Truth, I believe, will prevail. I want to see you face to face. Satan does not love that Christ's ministers should come together. I wish you could come up immediately, and stay at London whilst I am in the country: or rather go and preach at Bristol, Gloucester, and Wiltshire, for about a fortnight, and then come up to London. This, I believe, will be best. About that time, God willing, I shall return from Essex, and then we can consult what is best to be done for the cause of our dear master. O Jesus is love!

I am glad to hear brother Rowland is with you.[2] Go on in the strength of our dear Lord, and you shall see Satan like lightning fall from heaven.[3] Times are not yet dark enough for the dawning of a thorough reformation. At even-tide God speaks. My love to all that follow Jesus Christ with an unfeigned simplicity.[4] May the Lord hide your precious soul under the shadow of his almighty wings! Cease not to pray for

Yours eternally in Christ Jesus,
G.W.

1 *Works*, I, 268–269.

2 Daniel Rowland (1711–1790) was one of the main leaders of the revival in Wales. His ministry was mostly centred in North Wales. His ministry is not as well-known to English-speaking readers as that of Howel Harris. In large part this is because Rowland's literary remains are in Welsh. His extraordinarily powerful preaching led to his being nick-named "Boanerges," Son of Thunder (see Mark 3:17). In the words of Eifion Evans, his most recent biographer, "thousands flocked to hear him preach every Sunday, travelling vast distances and braving fierce persecution" ("Rowland, Daniel" in Lewis, ed., *Evangelical Biography*, II, 957–958). He was a very careful preacher, though. His personal library contained a number of works of the early Church Fathers as well as those from theologians of his own day. Rowland was careful, however, to attribute the power of his ministry wholly to the Spirit of God. As he once remarked: "If God does not pluck us, as brands out of the burning fire, by His free grace, and remove by His Spirit the veil of darkness and ignorance from our minds, none can be saved" [cited Eifion Evans, *Daniel Rowland and the Great Evangelical Awakening in Wales* (Edinburgh: The Banner of Truth Trust, 1985), 374]. For two full-length studies of Rowland, see John Owen, "A Memoir of Daniel Rowland of Llangeitho," *The Banner of Truth*, 215–216 (August–September 1981), 1–80; Evans, *Daniel Rowland and the Great Evangelical Awakening*.

3 Luke 10:18.

4 Compare Ephesians 6:24.

Jonathan Edwards
who, in September 1741, gave a well-known
commencement address on I John 4 to the students
at Yale College, New Haven

[Reprinted from Albert D. Belden, *George Whitefield —The Awakener* (London: Sampson Low, Marston & Co. Ltd., 1930), facing p.112]

19

To the Students, etc. under conviction at the Colleges of Cambridge and New Haven, in New England and Connecticut[1]

Dear Gentlemen,

A dead ministry will always make a dead people. Whereas, if ministers are warmed with the love of God themselves, they cannot but be instruments of diffusing that love among others. This, this is the best preparation for the work whereunto you are to be called. Learning without piety, will only make you more capable of promoting the kingdom of Satan. Henceforward, therefore, I hope you will enter into your studies not to get a parish, nor to be polite preachers, but to be great saints. This, indeed, is the most compendious way to true learning; for an understanding enlightened by the Spirit of God is more susceptible of divine truths, and I am certain will prove most useful to mankind. The more holy you are, the more will God delight to honour you. He loves to make use of instruments, which are like himself. I hope the good old divinity[2] will now be precious to your souls, and you will think it an honour to tread in the steps of your pious forefathers. They were acquainted with their own hearts. They knew what it was to be tempted themselves, and therefore from their own experience knew how to succour others. O may you follow them, as they followed Christ. Then great, very great will be your reward in heaven. I am sure you can never serve a better Master than Jesus Christ, or be engaged in a higher employ than in calling home souls to him. I trust, dear gentlemen, you will not be offended at me for sending you these few lines. I write out of the fullness of my heart. I make mention of you always in my prayers. Forget me not in yours. I am a poor weak worm. I am the chief of sinners,[3] and yet, O stupendous love! the Lord's work still prospers in my unworthy hands. Fail not to give thanks, as well as to pray for

Your affectionate brother and servant,

in our common Lord,

G.W.

[1] *Works*, I, 296–297. The colleges in view are those of Harvard and Yale, where Whitefield had preached in the autumn of 1740. See Dallimore, *George Whitefield*, I, 551–552.
[2] A reference to Puritan theology.
[3] 1 Timothy 1:15.

20

To the Rev. Mr. John Wesley [1]

Aberdeen
October 10, 1741

Reverend and dear Brother,

...I find I love you as much as ever, and pray God, if it be his blessed will, that we may be all united together. It hath been for some days upon my heart to write you, and this morning I received a letter from brother Harris,[2] telling me how he had conversed with you and your dear brother. May God remove all obstacles that now prevent our union! Though I hold particular election, yet I offer Jesus freely to every individual soul. You may carry sanctification to what degrees you will, only I cannot agree that the in-being of sin is to be destroyed in this life. O, my dear brother, the Lord hath been much with me in Scotland. I every morning feel my fellowship with Christ, and he is pleased to give me all peace and joy in believing. In about three weeks, I hope to be at Bristol. May all disputings cease, and each of us talk of nothing but Jesus, and him crucified! This is my resolution. The Lord be with your spirit. My love to brother Charles,[3] and all that love the glorious

Emmanuel. I am, without dissimulation,

Ever yours,
G.W.

1 *Works*, I, 331. For the background to this letter, see pp.52–58. This letter well reveals the catholicity of Whitefield and his desire to love all who loved the Lord Jesus in sincerity.
2 i.e. Howel Harris.
3 i.e. Charles Wesley.

21

To Mr. L– [1]

London, May 11, 1742

With this, I send you a few out of the many notes I
have received from persons, who were convicted,
converted, or comforted in Moorfields,[2] during the
late holidays. For many weeks, I found my heart
much pressed to determine to venture to preach
there at this season, when, if ever, Satan's children
keep up their annual rendezvous. I must inform you,
that Moorfields is a large spacious place, given, as I
have been told, by one Madam Moore, on purpose
for all sorts of people to divert themselves in. For
many years past, from one end to the other, booths
of all kinds have been erected, for mountebanks,
players, puppet shows, and such like. With a heart
bleeding with compassion for so many thousands led
captive by the devil at his will, on Whit-Monday,[3] at
six o'clock in the morning, attended by a large congregation of people, I ventured to lift up a standard
amongst them in the name of Jesus of Nazareth.

Perhaps there were about ten thousand in waiting, not for me, but for Satan's instruments to

Whitefield preaching at Moorfields in 1742

[Reprinted from *The Evangelical Library Bulletin*, 28 (Spring 1962), 10–11]

amuse them. Glad was I to find that I had for once as it were got the start of the devil. I mounted my field pulpit, almost all flocked immediately around it. I preached on these words, "As Moses lifted up the serpent in the wilderness, even so shall the Son of man be lifted up, etc."[4] They gazed, they listened, they wept; and I believe that many felt themselves stung with deep conviction for their past sins. All was hushed and solemn. Being thus encouraged, I ventured out again at noon; but what a scene! The fields, the whole fields seemed, in a bad sense of the word, all white, ready not for the Redeemer's, but Beelzebub's harvest. All his agents were in full motion, drummers, trumpeters, merry andrews,[5] masters of puppet shows, exhibitors of wild beasts, players, etc., all busy in entertaining their respective auditories. I suppose there could not be less than twenty or thirty thousand people. My pulpit was fixed on the opposite side, and immediately, to their great mortification, they found the number of their attendants sadly lessened. Judging that like saint Paul, I should now be called as it were to fight with beasts at Ephesus,[6] I preached from these words: "Great is Diana of the Ephesians."[7]

You may easily guess, that there was some noise among the craftsmen, and that I was honoured with having a few stones, dirt, rotten eggs, and pieces of dead cats thrown at me, whilst engaged in calling them from their favourite but lying vanities. My soul was indeed among lions; but far the greatest part of my congregation, which was very large, seemed for a while to be turned into lambs. This encouraged me to give notice that I would preach again at six o'clock in the evening.

I came, I saw, but what thousands and thousands more than before if possible, still more deeply engaged in their unhappy diversions; but some thousands amongst them waiting as earnestly to hear the gospel. This Satan could not brook. One of his choicest servants was exhibiting, trumpeting on a large stage; but as soon as the people saw me in my black robes and my pulpit, I think all to a man left him and ran to me. For a while I was enabled to lift up my voice like a trumpet, and many heard the joyful sound. God's people kept praying, and the enemy's agents made a kind of roaring at some distance from our camp. At length they approached nearer, and the merry andrew (attended by others, who complained that they had taken many pounds less that day on account of my preaching) got upon a man's shoulders, and advancing near the pulpit attempted to slash me with a long heavy whip several times, but always with the violence of his motion tumbled down. Soon afterwards, they got a recruiting serjeant with his drum, etc. to pass through the congregation. I gave the word of command, and ordered that way might be made for the king's officer. The ranks opened, while all march'd quietly through, and then closed again.

Finding those efforts to fail, a large body quite on the opposite side assembled together, and having got a large pole for their standard, advanced towards us with steady and formidable steps, till they came very near the skirts of our hearing, praying, and almost undaunted congregation. I saw, gave warning, and prayed to the captain of our salvation[8] for present support and deliverance. He heard and answered; for just as they approached us with looks full of resentment, I know not by what accident, they quarrelled among themselves, threw down their stuff and went their way, leaving however many of their company behind, who before we had done, I trust were brought over to join the besieged party. I think I continued in praying, preaching, and singing, (for the noise was too great at times to preach) about three hours. We then retired to the Tabernacle,[9] with my pockets full of notes from persons brought under concern, and read them amidst the praises and spiritual acclamation of thousands, who joined with the holy angels in rejoicing that so many sinners were snatched, in such an unexpected, unlikely place and manner, out of the very jaws of the devil. This was the beginning of the Tabernacle society. Three hundred and fifty awakened souls were received in one day, and I believe the number of notes exceeded a thousand; but I must have done, believing you want to retire to join in mutual praise and thanksgiving to God and the Lamb, with

Yours, etc.

G.W.

1 *Works*, I, 384–386. The identity of "Mr. L." is unknown.

2 At this period of time Moorfields was an eighteen-acre park in London. Whitefield gives a little of the history of the park in this letter. Dallimore describes it thus: "It was the site of the usual entertainments of the age—bear-baiting, merry-andrew shows, wrestling, cudgel playing and dog fights—and large numbers of people gathered there each evening and on Sundays to while away their hours at these diversions" (*George Whitefield*, I, 287).

3 Houghton notes that the reference to "Whit Monday" must be a mistake for Easter Monday. In 1742, Easter Monday fell on April 19, while Whit Monday was June 7, nearly a month after Whitefield wrote this letter. See also Tyerman, *George Whitefield*, I, 555, n.1. On the other hand, Edwin Welch believes Whitefield's reference to Whit Monday is accurate, for, according to Welch, he is actually describing events from Whit Monday, 1741. There are a few sources, including other passages from Whitefield's letters and the diary of Howel Harris, that seem to support this assertion. See *Two Calvinistic Methodist Chapels 1743–1811. The London Tabernacle and Spa Fields Chapel* (London: London Record Society, 1975), xiii–xiv.

4 John 3:14.

5 A "merry andrew" was a clown, a person who entertained other people by means of buffoonery.

6 See 1 Corinthians 15:32.

7 Acts 19:28.

8 i.e. Christ; see Hebrews 2:10 for the phrase.

9 The London Tabernacle, the nerve-centre of Calvinistic Methodism in the capital, was built in 1741 in the district of Moorfields. It lay to the west of what is now Tabernacle Street.

22

To Mr. L– [1]

London, May 15, 1742

My dear Friend,

Fresh matter of praise; bless ye the Lord, for he hath triumphed gloriously. The battle that was begun on Monday, was not quite over till Wednesday evening, though the scene of action was a little shifted. Being strongly invited, and a pulpit being prepared for me by an honest quaker, a coal merchant, I ventured on Tuesday evening to preach at Mary le bon fields,[2] a place almost as much frequented by boxers, gamesters, and such like, as Moorfields. A vast concourse was assembled together, and as soon as I got into the field pulpit, their countenance bespoke the enmity of their hearts against the preacher. I opened with these words, "I am not ashamed of the gospel of Christ, for it is the power of God unto salvation to every one that believeth."[3] I preached in great jeopardy; for the pulpit being high, and the supports not well fixed in the ground, it tottered every time I moved, and numbers of enemies strove to push my friends against the supporters, in order to throw me down.

But the Redeemer stayed my soul on himself, therefore I was not much moved, unless with compassion for those to whom I was delivering my master's message, which I had reason to think, by the strong impressions that were made, was welcome to many.

But Satan did not like thus to be attacked in his strongholds, and I narrowly escaped with my life; for as I was passing from the pulpit to the coach, I felt my wig and hat to be almost off. I turned about, and observed a sword just touching my temples. A young rake, as I afterwards found, was determined to stab me, but a gentleman, seeing the sword thrusting near me, struck it up with his cane, and so the destined victim providentially escaped. Such an attempt excited abhorrence; the enraged multitude soon seized him, and had it not been for one of my friends, who received him into his house, he must have undergone a severe discipline.

The next day, I renewed my attack in Moorfields, but would you think it? After they found that pelting, noise, and threatenings would not do, one of the merry andrews got up into a tree very near the pulpit, and shamefully exposed his nakedness before all the people. Such a beastly action quite abashed the serious part of my auditory; whilst hundreds of another stamp, instead of rising up to pull down the unhappy wretch, expressed their approbation by repeated laughs. I must own at first it gave me a shock; I thought Satan had now almost outdone himself; but recovering my spirits, I appealed to all, since now they have such a spectacle before them, whether I had wronged human nature in saying, after pious Bishop Hall, "that man, when left to himself, is half a devil and half a beast"; or as the great Mr. Law expressed himself, "a motley mixture of the beast and devil."[4] Silence and attention being thus gained, I concluded with a warm exhortation, and closed our festival enterprises, in reading fresh notes that were put up, praising and blessing God amidst thousands at the Tabernacle, for what he had done for precious souls, and on account of the deliverances he had wrought out for me and his people. I could enlarge; but being about to embark in the *Mary and Ann* for Scotland, I must hasten to subscribe myself,

Yours, etc.

G.W.

P.S. I cannot help but adding, that several little boys and girls who were fond of sitting round me on the pulpit, while I preached, and handing to me people's notes, though they were often pelted with eggs, dirt, etc. thrown at me, never once gave way; but on the contrary, every time I was struck, turned up their little weeping eyes, and seemed to wish they could receive the blows for me. God make them in the growing years great and living martyrs for him, who out of the mouth of babes and sucklings perfects praise![5]

1 *Works*, I, 387–388.

2 i.e. Marylebone Fields.

3 Romans 1:16.

4 "Pious Bishop Hall" is Joseph Hall (1574–1656). "Mr. Law" is William Law (1686–1761), whose *A Serious Call to a Devout and Holy Life* (1728) exercised a significant influence upon the early thought of John Wesley. See D.W. Bebbington, *Evangelicalism in Modern Britain. A History from the 1730s to the 1980s* (London: Unwin Hyman, 1989), 38. Wesley broke with Law, though, in 1739. Law's subsequent writings were strongly influenced by the obscure thought of the German mystic Jakob Boehme (1575–1624).

5 See Matthew 21:16.

23

To the Honourable Colonel Gardiner [1]

London, December 21, 1742

Honoured Sir,

Your kind letter put me in mind of righteous Lot, whose soul was grieved day by day at the ungodly conversation of the wicked.[2] It was the same with holy David. His eyes, like yours, honoured Sir, gushed out with water because men kept not God's law.[3] Let this be your comfort, honoured Sir, that ere long "the wicked shall cease from troubling you, and your weary soul shall be at rest." Our Saviour will give you a discharge, when you have fought a few more battles for him. An exceeding and eternal weight of glory is laid up for you, which God the righteous judge shall give you at that day.[4] I confess your situation and employment cannot be very agreeable to a disciple of the prince of peace.[5] But persons can better judge for themselves, than strangers can judge for them. However, I cannot say, I would change posts. Indeed, honoured sir, I think mine is a glorious employ. I am not ashamed of my master, though my master may well be ashamed of me. I know no other reason, why Jesus has put me into the ministry, than because I am the chief of sinners,[6] and therefore fittest to preach free grace to a world lying in the wicked one. Blessed be God, he gives much success, and for the generality answers your prayers, by giving me a thriving soul in a healthful body.

But O my unfruitfulness! I am often ashamed that I can do no more for that Jesus who hath redeemed me by his own most precious blood. Honoured Sir, the thoughts quite confound me. O that I could lie lower! Then should I rise higher. Could I take deeper root downwards, then should I bear more fruit upwards. I want to be poor in spirit.[7] I want to be meek and lowly in heart.[8] I want to have the whole mind that was in Christ Jesus.[9] Blessed be his name for what he has given me already. Blessed be his name, that out of his fulness I receive grace for grace.[10]

O that my heart was Christ's library! I would not have one thief to lodge in my Redeemer's temple. "Lord, scourge out every thief," is the daily language of my heart. The Lord will hear my prayer, and let my cry come unto him. I have just been writing to your honoured lady. I think she grows in grace. May you and yours be filled with all the fulness of God!

---

1 *Works*, I, 478–479. On James Gardiner, see "Appendix: The conversion of James Gardiner."
2 See 2 Peter 2:7.
3 See Psalm 119:136.
4 2 Corinthians 4:17; 2 Timothy 4:8.
5 Gardiner was a soldier.
6 1 Timothy 1:15.
7 See Matthew 5:3.

8 See Matthew 11:29.
9 See Philippians 2:5.
10 John 1:16.

Whitefield preaching in the open-air

[Reprinted from John Gillies, *Memoirs of Rev. George Whitefield* (New Haven: Horace Mansfield, 1834), facing p.40]

24

To Mr. J— S— [1]

Birmingham
December 31, 1743

My dear Friend,

What do you think? Since my last, I have stole a whole day to dispatch some private business; however, in the evening I expounded to a great room full of people, who would rush into my lodgings, whether I would or not. On Sunday morning at eight I preached in the street to about a thousand, with much freedom. I then went to church and received the sacrament, and afterwards preached to several thousands in the street. The hearers seemed much pleased and delighted. It happened by the providence of God that no minister would come to preach at a house at Wedgbury,[2] where a weekly lecture used to be kept up. I was therefore earnestly entreated to come. I went, after my afternoon's preaching at Birmingham, and preached there at six in the evening to many hundreds in the street. It is about six miles from Birmingham. The word came with power, and only one or two made a noise at a distance. Afterwards we had a precious meeting in private. The power of the dear Redeemer was much amongst us.

The person with whom I lodged was a widow fearing God. Her husband was an eminent saint, and had been refreshed by my writings, particularly my journals, as had many others that I met with. On Monday morning about eight I preached to a large company in a field. By eleven I returned to Birmingham, and preached to many thousands on a common near the town. The soldiers were exercising; but the officers hearing that I was coming to preach, dismissed them, and promised that no disturbance should be made. All was quiet, and a blessed time we had. In the afternoon about three I preached again to about the same company, with the same success.

Then I rode to Wedgbury and preached there, and afterwards exhorted; but I cannot well tell you, what a sweet melting time there was. Many were in tears. About one I went to bed exceeding happy. In the morning I broke up some fallow ground at a place called Mare-Green,[3] about two miles from Wedgbury. Much mobbing had been there against Mr. Wesley's friends.[4] A few poor souls began to insult me, but Jesus strengthened me much. Several clods were thrown, one of them fell on my head, and another struck my fingers, while I was in prayer. A sweet gospel spirit was given to me.

I preached again at Birmingham to larger auditories than before, about eleven the same morning and three in the afternoon. In the evening I expounded twice in a large room. Once to the rich, and once to the poor, and went to rest happier than the night before. In the morning I took my leave of the Birmingham people, who wept much and were indeed deeply affected, and shewed great concern at my departure. I then went to Kidderminster, about twelve miles from Birmingham, where I was kindly received by Mr. Williams,[5] with whom I have corresponded for near two years. Many friends were at his house. I was greatly refreshed to find what a sweet savour of good Mr. Baxter's doctrine, works and discipline remained to this day.[6]

> *The sweet remembrance of the just,*
> *Shall flourish when he sleeps in dust.*

I preached about three in the afternoon to a large auditory near the church. Some unkind men, though they promised not to do so, rang the bells; but our Saviour enabled me to preach with power. In the evening and next morning I preached in the meeting house. I then went with Mr. Williams to Bromsgrove, about seven miles from Kidderminster, and was kindly received by one Mr. K—y, a good man, and several others, among whom were two or three Baptist and one Independent ministers. About three in the afternoon I preached in a field. Some rude people kicked a football and sounded a horn at some distance, but the Lord enabled me to preach with boldness. About six I preached in the Baptist Meetinghouse,[7] left Kidderminster at eight, and reached Worcester about ten at night. Mr. Williams and another friend accompanied us.

...It is now near twelve. My dear friend, I wish you an exceeding happy new-year. This time twelve-month I was writing to you from Bristol. O what has the dear Lord Jesus done for me since that, and since I was born! And O what does he intend to do for me before I die, and when time shall be no more? I am lost in wonder! I must away and cry Grace! grace! Praying that you may be filled with all the fulness of God, I subscribe, my dearest friend,

Ever, ever yours whilst

G.W.

1 *Works*, II, 46–48.

2 i.e. Wednesbury. Whitefield's spelling of this word is probably influenced by the local pronunciation of it. See Tyerman, *George Whitefield*, II, 82.

3 i.e. Mayers Green.

4 On the violent riots that took place when John Wesley preached at Wednesbury in October 1743, see A. Skevington Wood, *The Burning Heart. John Wesley: Evangelist* (1967 ed.; repr. Minneapolis, Minnesota: Bethany House Publishers, 1978), 168–169.

5 On Joseph Williams, see p.22.

6 The crucial years of Richard Baxter's ministry at Kidderminster were from 1647 to 1661.

7 The Calvinistic Baptist cause in Bromsgrove had been founded in 1672 with John Eccles (d.1711) as it first pastor. By 1694 the church consisted of 130 members [*Joseph Ivimey*, *A History of the English Baptists* (London, 1814), II, 595–596]. George Yarnold, baptized in 1709 and appointed elder in 1716, was the church's third pastor. No records of his pastorate exist, but he appears to have still been the pastor in 1746. It seems most probable that it was Yarnold who invited

Whitefield to preach in the Baptist meeting-house. This incident is noteworthy, for very few English Calvinistic Baptists were supportive of Whitefield during his ministry. For this information regarding Yarnold, I am indebted to Sue Mills, Librarian/Archivist at the Angus Library, Regent's Park College, Oxford University, Oxford.

25

To Mr. D– T– [1]

Gloucester, February 9, 1744

My dear Friend,

Who knows what a day may bring forth? Last night I was called to sacrifice my Isaac,[2] I mean to bury my only child and son about four months old. Many things occurred to make me believe he was not only to be continued to me, but to be a preacher of the everlasting gospel. Pleased with the thought, and ambitious of having a son of my own, so divinely employed, Satan was permitted to give me some wrong impressions, whereby, as I now find, I misapplied several texts of Scripture. Upon these grounds I made no scruple of declaring, "that I should have a son, and that his name was to be John."[3] I mentioned the very time of his birth, and fondly hoped that he was to be great in the sight of the Lord. Every thing happened according to the predictions, and my wife having had several narrow escapes while pregnant, especially by her falling from a high horse, and my driving her into a deep ditch in a one-horse chaise a little before the time of her lying-in,[4] and from which we received little or no hurt, confirmed me in my expectation, that God would grant me my heart's desire. I would observe to you, that the child was even born in a room, which the master of the house had prepared as a prison for his wife for coming to hear me. With joy would she often look upon the bars and staples and chains which were fixed in order to keep her in. About a week after his birth, I publickly baptized him in the Tabernacle, and in the company of thousands solemnly gave him up to that God, who gave him to me. A hymn, too fondly composed by an aged widow, as suitable to the occasion, was sung,[5] and all went away big with hopes of the child's being hereafter to be employed in the work of God; but how soon are all their fond, and as the event hath proved, their ill-grounded expectations blasted, as well as mine.

House-keeping being expensive in London, I thought best to send both parent and child to Abergavenny, where my wife had a little house of my own,[6] the furniture of which, as I thought of soon embarking to Georgia, I had partly sold, and partly given away. In their journey thither, they stopped at Gloucester, at the Bell-Inn, which my brother now keeps, and in which I was born. There, my beloved was cut off with a stroke. Upon my coming here, without knowing what had happened, I enquired concerning the welfare of parent and child, and by the answer, found that the flower was cut down. I immediately called all to join in prayer, in which I blessed the Father of mercies for giving me a son, continuing it to me so long, and taking it from me so soon. All joined in desiring that I could decline preaching 'till the child was buried; but I remembered a saying of good Mr. [Matthew] Henry, "that weeping must not hinder sowing," and therefore preached twice the next day, and also the day following, on the evening of which, just as I was closing my sermon, the bell struck out for the funeral. At first, I must acknowledge, it gave nature a little shake, but looking up I recovered strength, and then concluded with saying, that this text on which I had been preaching, namely "all things worked together for good to them that love God,"[7] made me as willing to go out to my son's funeral, as to hear of his birth.

Our parting from him was solemn. We kneeled down, prayed, and shed many tears, but I hope tears of resignation. And then, as he died in the house wherein I was born, he was taken and laid in the church where I was baptized, first communicated, and first preached. All this you may easily guess threw me into very solemn and deep reflection, and I hope deep humiliation; but I was comforted from that passage in the book of Kings, where is recorded the death of the Shunammite's child, which the Prophet said, "The Lord had hid from him"; and the woman's answer likewise to the Prophet when he asked, "Is it well with thee? Is it well with thy husband? Is it well with thy child?" And she answered, "It is well."[8] This gave me no small satisfaction. I immediately preached upon the text the day following at Gloucester, and then hastened up to London, preached upon the same there; and though disappointed of a living preacher by the death of my son, yet I hope that what happened before his birth, and since at his death, hath taught me such lessons, as, if duly improved, may render his mistaken parent more cautious, more sober-minded, more experienced in Satan's devices, and consequently more useful in his future labours to the church of God. Thus, "out of the eater comes forth meat, and out of the strong comes forth sweetness."[9] Not doubting but our future life will be one continued explanation of this blessed riddle, I commend myself and you to the unerring guidance of God's Word and Spirit,[10] and am

Yours, etc.

G.W.

---

[1] *Works*, II, 50–52.

[2] A reference to God's command to Abraham to sacrifice his son Isaac in Genesis 22.

[3] Luke 1:13.

[4] An incident Whitefield related in Letter DXXXIV to Mrs. D—, September 2, 1743 (*Works*, II, 39–40).

[5] This hymn can be found in *Works*, II, 53.

[6] In November 1741 Whitefield had married a Welsh widow by the name of Elizabeth James (d.1768), who was some ten years older than he was. There were to be four miscarriages after the death of their infant son. On the nature of their marriage, see the judicious study by Dallimore, *George Whitefield*, II, 100–113, 471–473.

[7] Romans 8:28.

[8] 2 Kings 4:17–27.

[9] Judges 14:14, one of Whitefield's favourite texts.

[10] This remark is significant in view of his confession earlier

in the letter of the fallible nature of mental impressions. By contrast, God's Word is "unerring." Whitefield learned his lesson from this experience with his son. A couple of years later, in the sermon *Walking with God*, he would state, "always try the suggestions or impressions that you may at any time feel, by the unerring rule of God's most holy word" (*Sermons on Important Subjects*, 53).

John Cennick

26

To Mr. John Cennick [1]

New York, July 5, 1747

My dear John,

Though I am quite sick and weak in body, yet the love I owe thee for Jesu's sake, constrains me to answer your last kind letter, dated Febuary 5th. The other mentioned therein, never came to hand. I am sorry to hear there are yet disputings amongst us about brick-walls. I was in hopes, after our contests of that kind about seven years ago, [2] such a scene would never appear again; but I find fresh offences must come, to search out and discover to us fresh corruptions, to try our faith, teach us to cease from man, and to lean more upon him, who by his infinite wisdom and power will cause, "that out of the eater shall come forth meat, and from the strong sweetness." [3] I am glad you find yourself happy in the holy Jesus. I wish thee an increase of such dear-bought happiness every day, and pray that thy mouth may not be stopped, as others have been before thee, from publishing the glad tidings of salvation, by a crucified Redeemer. It has been thy meat and drink to preach among poor sinners the unsearchable riches of Jesus

Christ. May'st thou continue and abide in this plan, and whether I see thee or not, whether thou dost ever think of, or write to me any more, I wish thee much success, and shall always pray that the work of the Lord may prosper in thy hands.

Whether you have changed your principles with your situation, I know not. I would only caution thee against taking any thing for gospel upon the mere authority of man. Go where thou wilt, though thou shouldest be in the purest society under heaven, thou wilt find that the best of men are but men at the best, and will meet with stumbling blocks enough, to teach thee the necessity of a continual dependence on the Lord Jesus, who alone is infallible, and who will not give that glory to another. Blessed be his Name, for the trials I have met with from the friends of Zion. At present, I can rejoice in being deserted by one, and used unkind by another, who at the great day must own me to be their spiritual father. Such trials are very salutary. They lead me to the Cross, and I trust in the end will conform me to him, who in his bitterest agony had no one to watch with him, no not for one hour.

My dear man, you will excuse me, as my heart at present is affected with the thoughts of the divisions that subsist between the servants and churches of Jesus Christ. May Jesus heal them, and hasten that blessed time, when we shall all see eye to eye, and there shall be no disputings about houses, doctrine, or discipline in all God's holy mountain! God willing, I purpose seeing England next year, and shall be glad to converse with thee once more, about the things which belong to our Saviour's kingdom. If my present sickness ends in death, we shall converse in a better world, and without the least discord and contention....Jesus is yet with me, and causes my rod to bud and blossom. The bush burns, but is not consumed.[4] Adieu.

Thine in the glorious Emmanuel.

---

[1] *Works*, II, 113–114. For the identity of the recipient of this letter, see Tyerman, *George Whitefield*, II, 174. John Cennick (1718–1755) was one of the great evangelists of the Revival and a close friend of Whitefield. He joined the Moravians in 1745. On Cennick, see Peter J. Lineham, "Cennick, John" in Lewis, ed., *Evangelical Biography*, I, 210; *Life and Hymns of John Cennick*, ed. J.R. Broome (Harpenden, Hertfordshire: Gospel Standard Trust Publications, 1988).

[2] This is a reference to John Welsey's dismissal of John Cennick as the school master of the colliers' school at Kingswood in early 1741 during the doctrinal dispute between himself and Whitefield. For details, see Dallimore, *George Whitefield*, II, 38–40.

[3] Judges 14:14.

[4] An allusion to Exodus 3:2.

27

To the Rev. Mr. S— [1]

On board the Betsy
June 24, 1748

Rev. and very dear Sir,

Though we are about two hundred leagues from land, yet lest hurry of business should prevent me when we get ashore, I think proper to write you a few lines whilst I am on board. Long before this reaches you, I suppose you will have heard of what the Lord of all Lords was pleased to do for me and his people at, and also when we sailed from, [the] Bermudas. We sailed from thence just twenty-one days this morning, and have lived, as to the conveniences of eating and drinking, like people that came from the continent, rather than one of the islands, so bountiful were our friends, whom we left behind us. Hitherto we have met with no storms or contrary winds, only it begins to head us now. But God, in his own time, I trust will carry us to our desired port.

The first day we came out we were chased, and yesterday a large French vessel shot thrice at us and bore down upon us.[2] We gave up all for gone. I was dressing myself in order to receive our expected visitors. In the mean while, our Captain cries, "the danger is over." The Frenchman turned about and left us. He was quite near, and we almost defenceless. Now we are so near the [English] Channel, we expect such alarms daily. If any thing happens extraordinary, I shall be particular. As for other things, I cannot say much. The Captain is exceeding civil, and I have my passage free; but all I have been able to do in the great cabin in respect to religious duties, is to read the church prayers once every evening, and twice on the Lord's day. I have not preached yet; this may spare my lungs, but it grieves my heart. I long to be ashore, if it was for no other reason. Besides, I can do but little in respect to my writing. You may guess how it is, when we have four gentlewomen in the cabin. However, they have been, and are very civil, and I believe my being on board has been somewhat serviceable. My health I think is improved, and I have finished my abridgement of Mr. Law's *Serious Call*, which I have endeavoured to gospelize.[3] Yesterday I likewise made an end of revising all my journals. Blessed be God, for letting me have leisure to do it. I purpose to have a new edition before I see America.

Alas! Alas! In how many things have I judged and acted wrong. I have been too rash and hasty in giving characters, both of places and persons. Being fond of scripture language, I have often used a style too apostolical, and at the same time I have been too bitter in my zeal. Wild-fire has been mixed with it, and I find that I frequently wrote and spoke in my own spirit, when I thought I was writing and speaking by the assistance of the Spirit of God. I have likewise too much made inward impressions my rule of acting, and too soon and too explicitly published what had been better kept in longer, or told after my death. By these things I have given some wrong touches to God's ark, and hurt the blessed cause I would defend, and also stirred up needless opposition. This has humbled me much since I have been on board, and made me think of a saying of Mr. [Matthew] Henry's, "Joseph had more honesty than he had policy, or he never would have told his dreams."[4] At the same time, I cannot but bless, and praise, and magnify that good and gracious God, who filled me with so much of his holy fire, and carried me, a poor weak youth, through such a torrent both of popularity and contempt, and set so many seals to my unworthy ministrations. I bless him for ripening my judgment a little more, for giving me to see and confess, and I hope in some degree to correct and amend, some of my mistakes. I thank God for giving me grace to embark in such a blessed cause, and pray him to give me strength to hold on and increase in zeal and love to the end.

[1] *Works*, II, 143–145.
[2] England was at war with France and Spain for naval supremacy in the Atlantic and the Mediterranean. This was known as the War of the Austrian Succession (1740–1748).
[3] On William Law, see p.156, n.4,
[4] See Matthew Henry's comments on Genesis 37:9 [*Matthew Henry's Commentary On the Whole Bible* (Repr. Peabody, Massachusetts: Hendrickson Publishers, 1991), 1:170].

28

To Mr. C— [1]

London
July 12, 1748

My very dear Friend and Brother,

Though I am pretty much engaged, yet I cannot let your kind letter lie by me two posts unanswered. Blessed be God that you yet retain your simple heart, and are determined to know nothing but Jesus Christ and him crucified.[2] With this mind, may you climb up higher and higher in the Church of England, in order that you may move in a superior orb, and your light shine with greater and more diffusive ardor round the church of God!

O my dear Mr. C—, what has the Redeemer done for us! What is he still doing! It would gladden your heart to see what a turn affairs take in London. I have preached twice in St. Bartholomew's Church,[3] and helped to administer the sacrament once. I believe on Sunday we had a thousand communicants. Moorfields are as white as ever unto harvest, and multitudes flock to hear the Word. The old spirit of love and power seems to be revived amongst us. What am I, what am I, that Jesus Christ should still delight to honour me? O for a single eye and a simple heart unto the end!

By what I can judge, Satan will allure some with his golden bait. "In all times of our wealth, good Lord deliver us." Blessed be God, I am not much in danger of having too much of this world's goods at present. My outward affairs are yet behind hand. I long to owe no man any thing but love.[4]...Never mind me, let my name die every where, let even my friends forget me, if by that means the cause of the blessed Jesus may be promoted.[5]...My hearty respects await Mr. G—. I trust he determines to know nothing but Jesus Christ, and him crucified.[6] Commending you to his mercy, and myself to the continuance of your prayers, I subscribe myself, very dear Sir,

Yours eternally in the blessed Jesus, G.W.

1 *Works*, II, 150–151.

2 1 Corinthians 2:2.

3 This must be the Church of St. Bartholomew the Great, London, where Richard Thomas Bateman (1712–*c.*1760) was the rector. Bateman had known Whitefield in Oxford and came to identify himself fully with the revival.

4 See Romans 13:8.

5 In a letter to his friend James Hervey (1714–1758), Whitefield could say: "You judge right when you say, 'It is your opinion that I do not want to make a sect, or set myself at the head of a party.' No, let the name of Whitefield die, so that the cause of Jesus Christ may live" [Letter DCCXLVII, April 5, 1749 (*Works*, II, 248)].

6 1 Corinthians 2:2.

29

To Mr. T– [1]

London, December 21, 1748

Dear Mr. T—,

Have you not thought it unkind, that I answered not your letter before now. You will be pacified when I tell you, that not want of love but leisure hath been the cause of so long a silence. I will now redeem a few moments to pay this debt, and acknowledge a much greater debt of love that I owe, and intend indeed to be always owing to you and yours. Christ alone can pay you. He will. Whatever is done to his ministers, he looks upon as done to himself. What a blessed master do we serve! Thanks be to his great name, he continues to deal lovingly with me. I have been blessed in my late excursion into the country, and likewise since I came to town. The prospect of doing good at least to some of the rich, is very encouraging. I know you will pray, that the foolishness of preaching may be a means of bringing some of them to believe on him who justifies the ungodly.[2] You find, that not gifts but grace, sovereign, all powerful grace alone, can reach the hearts.

...I am now thirty-four years of age. Little did I

think of living so long. And yet when I consider how I have lived, shame and confusion cover my face. O my dear Mr. T—, as you are preparing for the ministry, lose not one moment of time, but labour to be always on the stretch for him, who was stretched on the accursed cross for you. Study books and men, but above all, study your own heart and the knowledge of Jesus Christ, and him crucified.[3] Get your heart free from worldly hopes and worldly fears, and you will avoid thousands of those snares, into which young ministers for want of this too often fall. O let the language of your heart be, "God forbid that I should glory, save in the cross of Christ, by whom the world is crucified unto me and I unto the world."[4] You will excuse this freedom. It proceeds from the love I bear you.

[1] *Works*, II, 216–217.
[2] See Romans 4:5.
[3] 1 Corinthians 2:2.
[4] Galatians 6:14.

30

To Lady Huntingdon [1]

Plymouth
February 16, 1749

Honoured Madam,

The last time I wrote to your Ladyship, I was at Exeter, where I begun on Sunday evening to preach in the open air. Abundance of souls attended, and I trust real good was done. In the morning, grace flowed richly round the congregation; and many knew experimentally that Christ was risen, by his giving them to experience the power of his resurrection in their hearts. On Monday I went to Bovey Tracey, about 12 miles from Exeter, where I found several poor simple souls. Here also the fountain of life was open, and I believe some drank at, and others felt the want of it. The next morning, I preached at a place called Mary-Church, where are supposed to be near a score of awakened souls, who have undergone much outward trouble for adhering to the cross of Christ. Most of their bitterest opposers were present. All was calm; and the power of the Lord accompanied the Word.

After sermon I rode twenty miles to Kingsbridge,

Selina Hastings,
the Countess of Huntingdon

where, to my great surprise, I found about a thousand souls waiting till eight in the evening to hear the Word. Though nature said, "Spare thyself," I thought faith and duty said, "Venture upon the Lord's strength, and speak to them." I did, from these words of our dear Lord's: "I must work the works of him that sent me, while it is day: the night cometh when no man can work."[2] I preached in the street. The moon shone. All was quiet; and I hope some begun to think of working out their salvation with fear and trembling.[3] The next morning I preached there again; four ministers attended. Our Lord was pleased to make it a very fine season. After sermon I had the pleasure of hearing, that by two or three discourses preached at this place about 5 years ago, many souls were awakened. One young man, then called, is since a preacher; he was in a tree partly to ridicule me. I spoke to him to imitate Zaccheus, and come down and receive the Lord Jesus. The Word was backed with power. He heard, came down, believed, and now adorns the gospel.

From Kingsbridge to Plymouth, is near twenty post miles. Hither I came last night. About ten miles from the town, I met several of my spiritual children, who came on horseback to see me. When I came into the town, many hundreds were waiting to hear the Word, and received me with great joy. Though it was past seven at night, and I had preached at Kingsbridge in the morning, I thought it my duty to comply with the people's importunity, and accordingly I called upon them, (in a place

187

styled after the Tabernacle, built since I have been absent) to behold the Lamb of God.[4] I find a strange alteration in the people since I came first here, now above four years ago. Many were then awakened, and truly converted to the blessed Jesus. I write in a house belonging to a married couple, who call me their spiritual father.[5] Plymouth seems to be quite a new place to me. I have also just now parted from a truly converted neighbouring clergyman, who has invited me to preach in his church. Ere long I hope to send your Ladyship some more good news.

[1] *Works*, II, 230–231. Selina Hastings (1707–1791), the Countess of Huntingdon, had been converted in the autumn of 1739 and in time became a leading figure in the advance of the revival. In the doctrinal differences between Whitefield and the Wesleys, she initially took the side of the latter. By 1748, though, she had embraced the doctrines of grace and appointed Whitefield as her chaplain. This gave the evangelist excellent opportunities to witness to members of the English aristocracy, and a number were converted. During the 1760s, at her own expense, she began to erect chapels for the preaching of the gospel where parish ministers were not sympathetic to the revival. Eventually in 1780 these chapels and preaching posts, which numbered close to seventy, separated from the Anglican Church and she found herself the head of a denominational body, the Countess of Huntingdon's Connexion. When she died, she had spent her entire fortune for the furtherance of the gospel and was £3,000 in debt, but was full of such plans as the conversion of the Jews and the sending of missions to such places as Paris and Madrid, and even Tahiti. She had a remarkable ministry, though it was sometimes hampered by her dominating personality. For two recent studies of her life, see Edwin Welch,

Spiritual Pilgrim: A Reassessment of the Life of the Countess of Huntingdon (Cardiff: University of Wales Press, 1995) and Boyd Stanley Schlenther, *Queen of the Methodists: The Countess of Huntingdon and the Eighteenth-Century Crisis of Faith and Society* (Durham: Academic Press, 1997). For two briefer studies, see John R. Tyson, "Lady Huntingdon's Reformation," *Church History*, 64 (1995), 580–593; *idem*, "Lady Huntingdon and the Church of England," *The Evangelical Quarterly*, 72 (2000), 23–34.

2 John 9:4.

3 An allusion to Philippians 2:12.

4 John 1:29.

5 This was the house of Andrew Kinsman (1725–1793), a grocer, and his wife Ann. Both Andrew and Ann had been converted under Whitefield's preaching. Kinsman eventually became the minister of the Tabernacle in Plymouth. See Edwin Welch, "Andrew Kinsman's Churches at Plymouth," *Report and Transactions of the Devonshire Association for the Advancement of Science, Literature and Art*, 97 (1965), 212–236.

31

To the Countess of Delitz [1]

Plymouth, February 22, 1749

Honoured Madam,

Yesterday I had the favour of your Ladyship's letter, which I would have answered immediately, but was engaged both in company, and in preaching the everlasting gospel. Your Ladyship's answering my poor scrawl was an honour I did not expect; but, since your Ladyship is pleased thus to condescend, I am encouraged to make a reply. And give me leave to assure your Ladyship, that your own case, and that of your honoured sisters, have been, and are always upon my heart. I pray for both in public and private, though none knows whom I mean. Blessed be the God and Father of our Lord Jesus Christ, who, I trust, hath imparted a saving knowledge of his eternal Son to your Ladyship's heart. Your letter bespeaks the language of a soul which hath tasted that the Lord is gracious,[2] and hath been initiated into the divine life. Welcome, thrice welcome, honoured Madam, into the world of new creatures! O what a scene of happiness lies before you! Your frames, my Lady, like the moon, will wax and wane;

but the Lord Jesus, on whose righteousness you solely depend, will, notwithstanding, remain your faithful friend in heaven. Your Ladyship seems to have the
right point in view, to get a constant abiding witness
and indwelling of the blessed Spirit of God in your
heart. This the Redeemer has purchased for you. Of
this he has given your Ladyship a taste; this, I am
persuaded, he will yet impart so plentifully to your
heart, that out of it shall flow rivers of living waters.
This Jesus spake of the Spirit, which they that believe
on him should receive.[3] As you have, therefore, honoured Madam, received the Lord Jesus, so walk in
him even by faith.[4] Lean on your beloved, and you
shall go on comfortably through this howling
wilderness, till you arrive at those blissful regions,

Where pain, and sin, and sorrow cease,
And all is calm, and joy, and peace.

---

[1] *Works*, II, 236–237. Louise Sophie von der Schulenburg
(1692–1773), the Countess of Delitz, was the illegitimate
daughter of George I by one of his mistresses, Melusina von
der Schulenburg (1667–1743), the Countess of Kendal. She
was married and divorced before 1714. Witty and beautiful,
Louise consorted with a series of lovers before being caught
by her husband *in flagrante*. He divorced her. In the grace of
God, though, she was converted, as this letter bears witness.
See Ragnhild Hatton, *George I: Elector and King* (London:
Thames and Hudson, 1978), 136–137.

[2] Psalm 34:8.

[3] John 7:38–39.

[4] Colossians 2:6.

32

To Mr. S– [1]

London, March 11, 1749

My very dear Mr. S—,

I wish you joy. I trust you may now say, "Now I begin to be a disciple of Jesus Christ." You know who has commanded us to rejoice and be exceeding glad when men separate from our company, and speak all manner of evil against us falsely for his name's sake.[2] Thanks be to God, you have at length found out, that whosoever attempts to reconcile God and the world, is attempting to reconcile two irreconcilable differences. They are as opposite as light and darkness, heaven and hell. You have nothing to do, but to go on doing, and then sing with an holy triumph,

> *For this let men revile my name,*
> *I shun no cross, I fear no shame;*
> *All hail reproach, and welcome pain,*
> *Only thy terrors, Lord, restrain.*

You know he is faithful, who hath promised, "that he will never leave nor forsake you."[3] Wait on him therefore, dear Sir, and you shall renew your strength, nay you shall mount on wings like an eagle; you shall walk and not be weary, you shall run and not be faint.[4] Various are the trials inward and outward that you will meet with. It is in the spiritual as in the natural birth. The after-pangs are sometimes sharper than those that precede the new-birth itself. If you are made use of by Jesus Christ, no wonder that Satan desires to have you, that he may sift you as wheat. But fear not; Jesus prays for you; your faith therefore shall not fail.[5] How was Paul humbled and struck down before he was sent forth to preach the everlasting gospel? Prayer, temptation, and meditation, says Luther, are necessary ingredients for a minister. If God teaches us humility, it must be as Gideon taught the men of Succoth, by thorns.[6]

...Why we should not press after and continually plead for assurance, which is every where through the holy Scriptures spoken of as the common portion of God's children, I cannot yet see. It is a false humility to be content without that which God offers and promises to give. Let him give it in his own way and time; but, "Lord give me a full assurance of faith, that I may joy and rejoice in thee evermore!" should be the constant cry of your soul.

---

1 *Works*, II, 245–246.
2 A reference to Jesus' statement in Matthew 5:11.
3 Hebrews 13:5.
4 Isaiah 40:31.
5 Luke 22:31–32.
6 See Judges 8:5–16.

33

To the Rev. Mr. William Grimshaw [1]

London, March 17, 1749

My dear Brother,

What a blessed thing it is that we can write to, when we cannot see one another! By this means we increase our joys, and lessen our sorrows, and, as it were, exchange hearts.[2]

Thanks be to the Lord Jesus that the work flourishes with you! I am glad your children grow so fast; they become fathers soon; I wish some may not prove dwarfs at last. A word to the wise is sufficient. I have always found awakening times like spring times. Many blossoms, but not always so much fruit. But go on, my dear man, and, in the strength of the Lord, you shall do valiantly. I long to be your way; but I suppose it will be two months first.

Pray tell my dear Mr. Ingham[3] that I cannot now answer the Preston letter,[4] being engaged in answering a virulent pamphlet, entitled, *The Enthusiasm of the Methodists and Papists compared*, supposed to be done by the Bishop of Exeter.[5] Thus it must be. If we will be temple builders, we must have the temple builders' lot; I mean, hold a sword in one hand, and

William Grimshaw

a trowel in the other.[6] The Lord make us faithful Nehemiahs, for we have many Sanballats to deal with! But, wherefore should we fear? If Christ be for us, who can be against us?[7]

...My dear brother, good night. May the Lord Jesus be with your spirit, and make you wise to win souls, even as wise as an angel of God! Remember me in the kindest manner, to honest-hearted Mr. Ingham, and tell him that, in a post or two, I hope he will hear from

His and your most affectionate though unworthy Brother and fellow-labourer in Christ's vineyard, G.W.

---

[1] *Works*, II, 246–247. For the identification of the recipient of this letter, see Tyerman, *George Whitefield*, II, 218–219. William Grimshaw (1708–1763) was an "ungodly cleric" when he went to the village of Todmorden, Yorkshire, as the parish curate. After much soul-searching and pondering of a couple of Puritan classics by Thomas Brooks (1608–1680) and John Owen (1616–1683), he was converted there in 1741. Roughly a year after his conversion he had moved to nearby Haworth, famous in our day for being the home of the nineteenth-century Brontës, but in Grimshaw's day it was a spiritual wilderness, largely devoid of the life-transforming message of the gospel. When Grimshaw arrived at the parish church, there were but twelve who regularly came forward for the Lord's Supper. By the summer of 1747 that number had risen to the astonishing figure of twelve hundred as the result of a marvellous outpouring of the Holy Spirit. There was a cost, though—a punishing, physical toll on Grimshaw's bodily strength as he sought to preach throughout the area around Haworth. There was also persecution, at times violent and brutal. But as Faith Cook notes

in her recent biography of Grimshaw, he counted all the hardship he suffered for Jesus, his dear Redeemer, as nothing in light of what Christ had done for him. Cook's recent study of Grimshaw's life and ministry is indispensable reading for anyone interested in the eighteenth-century Evangelical Revival: *William Grimshaw of Haworth* (Edinburgh: The Banner of Truth Trust, 1997).

2   This remark provides an excellent insight into Whitefield's view of the spiritual value of letter-writing.

3   Whitefield had known Benjamin Ingham (1712–1772) since his days at Oxford. Ingham went to America with the Wesley brothers in 1736, and it was there that he was converted prior to his return to England in 1737. He married Lady Margaret Hastings (1700–1768), Selina Hastings' sister-in-law, in 1741. They made their home in Yorkshire and from there Ingham exercised an itinerant preaching ministry in the West Riding, Lancashire and Westmoreland. In 1742 Ingham joined the Moravians, but by 1754 he, and about eighty congregations, withdrew from the Moravians to form their own loose connection of Inghamites. For an excellent study of Ingham's life, see H.M. Pickles, *Benjamin Ingham: Preacher amongst the Dales of Yorkshire, the Forests of Lancashire, and the Fells of Cumbria* (Coventry, 1995).

4   "The Preston letter" was a sermon by George White, the Anglican minister at Colne, Lancashire, in which White attacked Whitefield's honesty. Whitefield never did answer it. It was Grimshaw who wrote an "octavo book of ninety-eight pages" in response to White's work. See Tyerman, *George Whitefield*, II, 218–219; Cook, *William Grimshaw*, 126–127, 133–137.

5   Whitefield's response to this pamphlet by George Lavington (1684–1762), the Bishop of Exeter, appeared within the year as *Some Remarks on a Pamphlet entitled, The Enthusiasm of the Methodists and Papists compar'd* (London: W. Strahan, 1749).

6   This is an allusion to the rebuilding of the Temple after the Exile, as is the following sentence; see Nehemiah 4,

especially verses 17–18.
7   Romans 8:31.

Whitefield assaulted by a mob in Dublin, Ireland (1757)

[Reprinted from John Gillies, *Memoirs of Rev. George Whitefield* (New Haven: Horace Mansfield, 1834), facing p.168]

34

To Colonel Gumley [1]

February 8, 1750

My very dear C—,

Your kind letter reached me this day, just as I came out of the country from preaching the everlasting gospel, and where the blessed Redeemer was pleased to visit and greatly refresh his people. Last Monday we had a like feast; and in this place the Word has been attended with an alarming and quickening power. Contrary to my intentions, I have been prevailed on to stay all this week; so that I do not expect to be at Bristol till Monday or Tuesday next. A letter, if you are pleased to favour me with another, may find me there next week. I am sorry to hear you are ill of an ague; but this, and every thing we meet with here, is only to shake and free us of our corruptions, and to fit us more and more for a blessed hereafter. As long as we are below, if we have not one thing to exercise us, we shall have another. Our trials will not be removed, but only changed. Sometimes troubles come from without, sometimes from within, and sometimes from both together. Sometimes professed enemies, and sometimes nearest and dearest friends, are suffered to attack us. But Christ is the believer's hollow square;[2] and if we keep close in that, we are impregnable. Here only I find my refuge. Garrisoned in this, I can bid defiance to men and devils. Let who will thwart, desert, or over-reach, whilst I am in this strong-hold, all their efforts, joined with the prince of darkness, to disturb or molest me, are only like the throwing of chaff against a brass wall.

O my dear Sir, what did I experience on the road this day! How did I rejoice at the prospect of a judgement to come, and in the settled conviction, that, to the best of my knowledge, I have no designs, no views, but to spend and be spent for the good of precious and immortal souls. O that I may be content to be poor, to make others rich.[3] O that I may never be suffered to seek my own things, but the things of the Lord Jesus![4] His hand, without adding our carnal policy to it, will support his own cause, and make it more than conqueror over all. When fleshly wisdom, carnal reason, or human cunning is made use of, what is it, but, like Uzza, to give a wrong touch to God's ark, and in the end provoke God to smite us?[5]

I love you, dear Sir, because I hope and believe you have a tenderness for all that belong to Jesus. I pray God to increase this spirit in you. For what we lose of this, so much we lose of heaven, and so far are we destitute of the mind that was and is in Jesus. A bigoted, sectarian, party spirit cometh not from above, but is sensual, earthly, devilish.[6] Many of

God's children are infected with it; but then they are sick of a bad distemper. May the Spirit of God convince and cure them!

But whither am I running? Excuse, dear Sir, the overflowings of a heart, at present, I hope, filled with the love of God. It is free, unmerited, distinguishing, infinite love, or it would never flow into my ungrateful soul....Are we not as brands plucked out of the burning?[7] Free grace! Free grace! I hope to spend an eternity with you in praising the Lord of all lords for it.

---

[1] *Works*, II, 324–326. Colonel Gumley had been converted under Whitefield's preaching at one of the Countess of Huntingdon's residences. See Tyerman, *George Whitefield*, II, 249.

[2] On this metaphor, see pp.48–49.

[3] See 2 Corinthians 8:9.

[4] See Philippians 2:4,21.

[5] See 1 Chronicles 13:9–10.

[6] James 3:15. Whitefield is clearly thinking of the next verse as well, where James writes: "For where envying and strife *is*, there *is* confusion and every evil work (KJV)." In Whitefield's view, the strife between different denominational bodies is rooted in "earthly, sensual, devilish" thinking.

[7] See Zechariah 3:2.

Rowland Hill

35

To Rowland Hill [1]

London, July 21, 1767

My dear Sir,

I hope, ere this comes to hand, you will have taken your second degree. A good degree indeed: to be a preacher, a young preacher, a mobbed, perhaps a stoned preacher—O what an honour! How many prayers will you get when I read your letter at Tabernacle; and the prayers of so many dear children of God will do you no hurt, I assure you. When we are fighting with Amalek below, it is good to have a Joshua praying for us above.[2] Jesus is our Joshua, Jesus is our intercessor; he liveth, he ever liveth to make intercession,[3] especially for his young soldiers. Yonder, yonder he sits, whilst praying he reaches out a crown; at this distance you may see written in capital letters, VINCENTI DABO.[4] All a gift, a free gift, though purchased by his precious blood.

Tell churchmen, tell meetingers,[5] tell the wounded, tell all of this; tell them when you are young, you may not live to be old; tell them whilst you are an undergraduate, you may be dead, buried, glorified, before you take a college degree; tell those

Tottenham Court Chapel, built for Whitefield in 1756

who would have you spare yourself, that time is short, that eternity is endless, that the Judge is before the door: but I can no more,—the thought overwhelms. But with what? With joy, joy unspeakable and full of glory.[6] Good night!…God bless you! God bless you!

---

1 *Works*, III, 349–350. For the identification of Hill as the recipient of this letter, see Tyerman, *George Whitefield*, II, 529–530. In the early years of the nineteenth century, Rowland Hill (1744–1833) was one of the most important and popular evangelical preachers in England. In the view of the Countess of Huntingdon, "excepting my beloved and lamented Mr. Whitefield, I never witnessed any person's preaching where there was [sic] such displays of the Divine power and glory as in Mr. Hill's" [cited *The Life and Times of Selina, Countess of Huntingdon* (London: William Edward Painter, 1840), I, 211]. C.H. Spurgeon attests to his significance when he declares in his sermon *The Holy Ghost the Need of the Age*, preached on 13 March 1887: "I am not among those who despair for the good cause; but certainly I would be glad to see the Elishas who are to succeed the Elijah's who have gone up. Oh, for another Calvin or Luther! Oh, for a Knox or a Latimer, a Whitefield or a Wesley! Our fathers told us of Romaine and Newton, Toplady and Rowland Hill: where are the like of these?" [repr. *Spurgeon Ministries*, 21 (May 1988), 8]. For brief studies of his ministry, see Michael A.G. Haykin, "Rowland Hill: Some Anecdotes," *The Banner of Truth*, 317 (February 1990), 17–22; Stanley Jebb, "Rowland Hill, Eccentric Evangelist" in *The Fire Divine* (London: The Westminster Conference, 1996), 111–138.

2 This appears to be a reference to Exodus 17, where Israel fought the Amalekites. But it was Moses who prayed and Joshua who did battle.

3 See Hebrews 7:25.

4 i.e. "I will give to the one who overcomes."

5 i.e. Dissenters. This noun is obviously derived from the fact that the Dissenters worshipped in what they called "meetinghouses."

6 See 1 Peter 1:8.

36

A prayer of one desiring to be awakened to an experience of the new birth [1]

Blessed Jesus, thou hast told us in thy Gospel, that unless a man be born again of the Spirit, and his righteousness exceed the outward righteousness of the scribes and Pharisees, he cannot in any wise enter into the Kingdom of God. Grant me therefore, I beseech thee, this true circumcision of the heart; and send down thy blessed Spirit to work in me that inward holiness which alone can make me meet to partake of the heavenly inheritance with the saints in light.

Create in me, I beseech thee, a new heart, and renew a right spirit within me. For of whom shall I seek for succour but of thee, O Lord, with whom alone this is possible? Lord if thou wilt thou canst make me whole. O say unto my soul as thou didst once unto the poor leper, I will, be thou renewed. Have compassion on me, O Lord, as thou once hadst unto blind Bartimeus, who sat by the wayside begging.

Lord, thou knowest all things, thou knowest, what I would have thee to do. Grant, Lord, that I may receive my sight. For I am conceived and born in sin, my whole head is sick, my whole heart is faint, from the crown of my head to the sole of my feet I am full of wounds and bruises and putrifying sores. And yet I see it not. O awaken me, though it be with thunder, to a sensible feeling of the corruptions of my fallen nature. And for thy mercy's sake suffer me no longer to sit in darkness and the shadow of death.

O prick me, prick me to the heart! Dart down a ray of that all-quickening light which struck thy servant Saul to the ground, and make me cry out with the trembling jailer, "What shall I do to be saved?"

Lord, behold I pray, and blush, and am confounded that I never prayed on this wise before.

But I have looked upon myself as rich, not considering that I was poor and blind, and naked. I have trusted to my own righteousness. I flattered myself I was whole, and therefore blindly thought I had no need of thee, O great Physician of souls, to heal my sickness.

But being now convinced by thy free mercy that my own righteousness is as filthy rags, and that he is only a true Christian who is one inwardly; behold, with strong cryings and tears, and groanings that cannot be uttered, I beseech thee, visit me with thy free Spirit, and say unto these dry bones, "Live."

I confess, O Lord, that thy grace is thy own, and that thy Spirit bloweth where he listeth. And wast thou to deal with me after my deserts, and reward me according to my wickedness, I had long since been given over to a reprobate mind, and had my conscience seared as with a red-hot iron.

But, O Lord, since by sparing me so long thou hast shewn that thou wouldst not the death of a sinner. And since thou hast promised that thou wilt give thy Holy Spirit to those that ask it, I hope thy goodness and long-suffering is intended to lead me to repentance, and that thou wilt not turn away thy face from me.

Thou seest, O Lord, thou seest, that with the utmost earnestness and humility of soul, I ask thy Holy Spirit of thee, and am resolved in confidence of thy promise, who canst not lie, to seek and knock till I find a door of mercy opened unto me.

Lord save me, or I perish. Visit, O visit me with thy Salvation. Lighten my eyes, that I sleep not in death. O let me no longer continue a stranger to myself. But quicken me, quicken me with thy free Spirit that I may know myself even as I am known.

Behold here I am. Let me do and suffer what seemeth good in thy sight, only renew me by thy Spirit in my mind, and make me a partaker of thy divine nature. So shall I praise thee all the days of my life, and give thee thanks for ever in the glories of thy kingdom, O most adorable Redeemer, to whom with the Father and the Holy Ghost, be ascribed all honour and praise both now and for evermore. Amen.

1 This prayer and the two that follow are taken from George Whitefield, *Sermons on Various Subjects* (London: James Hutton, 1739), volume II. This volume actually has six prayers that appear to have been composed by Whitefield and that come at the end of the volume (pp.129–150). These prayers are a precious window into Whitefield's own soul and piety. This prayer for a person desiring to be saved can be found on pp.145–147. Unlike the letters, biblical references and allusions have not been identified in the prayers.

37

A prayer for one under the displeasure of relations for being religious [1]

Blessed Lord, who hast commanded us to call upon thee in time of trouble, and thou wilt deliver us; and hast always shewn thyself to be a God hearing Prayer, mighty and willing to save; hear me now, I pray thee, when I call upon thee, for trouble is at hand.

Thou seest, O Lord, how many of my brethren according to the flesh persecute me for thy Name's sake, so that I must renounce them, or decline openly professing thee before men.

But God forbid I should love father or mother, brethren or sisters more than thee, and thereby prove myself not worthy of thee. No! I have long since given thee my soul and my body. So lo! I now freely give thee my friends also.

For I now find by experience that as it was formerly, so it is now: they that are born after the flesh do persecute those that are born after the Spirit; that thou camest not to send peace on earth, but a sword; and that, unless a man forsake all that he hath, he cannot be thy disciple.

Lo! I come to perform this part of thy will, O my

God, being assured, that whosoever forsaketh father or mother, brethren or sisters, houses or lands for thy Sake or the Gospel shall receive a hundred-fold in this present life, with persecution, and in the world to come life everlasting.

I trust, O Lord, it is for [thy] sake alone that I now make an offering of the favour of my friends to thee; for thou knowest, O Lord, how continually they cry out, Spare thyself, tho' I am doing no more than thy holy Word strictly requires me to do.

But do thou, O blessed Saviour, who saidst unto Peter, "Get thee behind me Satan," enable me to stop my ears to their false insinuations, charm they never so sweetly; for they favour not the things that be of God, but the things that be of men. And unless, O Lord, thou dost help, they will be an offence unto me and cause me to deny the Lord that bought me.

Far be it from me, O Lord, to be surprised, because of those offences; for thou hast long since denounced woe against the world because of offences; and, I find, it is needful for my soul that such offences should come, to try what is in my heart. And try whether I love thee in deed and in truth.

Blessed, therefore, forever blessed be thy holy Name that I am accounted worthy to suffer for thy Name's sake. O let me rejoice and be exceeding glad that my reward shall be great in heaven.

O let me never regard any of their threatenings, for when my father and mother forsaketh me, thou, O Lord, I am assured, wilt take me up.

Take me, O take me into thy arms of thy mercy, for henceforward know I no man after the flesh. And whosoever doth the will of my Father, the same shall be my brother, and sister, and mother.

I know, O Lord, I know, that this will expose me to the derision and persecution of those that are round about me.

But do thou, who didst seek for the poor beggar, after he was cast out by the Jewish council, and didst reveal thyself unto him, reveal thyself to me also, when my name is cast out as evil by my friends and the world. Though they curse, yet bless thou me, O Lord, and enable me, I most humbly beseech thee, to pray for them, even when they most despitefully use me, and persecute me. Father forgive them, for they know not what they do.

It is owing, O Lord, to thy free mercy alone, that I have in any measure been enlightened to know thee and the power of thy resurrection. O let the same grace be sufficient for them also, and make thy almighty power to be known in their conversion.

Thou didst once, O blessed Saviour, magnify thy goodness in turning thy servant Paul from being a bitter persecutor to be a zealous preacher of thy Gospel; and madest the trembling jailer cry out, even to those whose feet he had hurt in the stocks, "Sirs, what shall I do to be saved?"

Look down, therefore, I beseech thee, in pity and compassion, on those of my own household; and after I am converted myself, make me, or some other, instrumental, to strengthen these my weak brethren;

that tho' we are now divided amongst ourselves, two against three, and three against two, yet we may at last, all with one heart and one mouth, glorify thee, O Lord; that thou mayst come and abide with us, and love us as thou didst [love] Lazarus, Mary, and her sister Martha. Grant this, O Saviour, for thy infinite merit's sake. Amen and Amen.

1 Whitefield, *Sermons on Various Subjects*, 141–144.

38

A prayer for one entrusted with the education of children [1]

O dearest Jesu, who gatherest thy lambs into thy bosom, and didst solemnly command thy servant Peter, to feed thy lambs, grant that I may shew that I love thee more than all things by doing as thou hast commanded him.

Lord, who am I, or what is in me, that thou should thus put honour upon me in making me any way instrumental to the preparing of souls for thee? O Saviour, I have sinned against heaven and am no more worthy to be called thy son, much less to be employed in the service of thy children.

But since thou hast been pleased in me to shew forth all thy mercy, and hast called me by thy good providence to this blessed work, grant that I may always remember that the little flock committed to my charge are bought with the price of thy own most precious blood. And let it therefore be my meat and drink to feed them with the sincere milk of thy Word that they may grow thereby.

To this end, I beseech thee of thy free grace, first to convert my own soul, and cause me to become like a little child myself, that from an experimental knowledge of my own corruptions, I may have my spiritual senses exercised to discern the first emotions of evil that may at any time arise in their hearts.

Oh give me, I beseech thee, a discerning spirit that I may search, and try, and examine the different tempers of their sin-sick souls; and, like a skillful physician, apply healing or corrosive medicines as their respective maladies shall require.

Gracious Jesus, let punishing be always my strange work; and, if it be possible, grant that they may be all drawn to their duty, as I would be drawn myself, by the cords of love. And when I am obliged to correct them, grant it may not be to shew my authority, or gratify a corrupt passion, but purely out of the same motive from which thou dost correct us, to make them partakers of thy holiness.

Oh! keep me, I beseech thee, from being angry without a cause. Permit me not rashly to be provoked by the infirmities and perverseness of their infant years; but grant I may shew all longsuffering towards them. And by exercising such frequent acts of patience and forbearance, grant, I myself may learn the meekness and gentleness of Christ.

O thou, who taughtest thy disciples how to pray, pour down, I beseech thee, the Spirit of grace and supplication into their hearts that at all times and in all places they may both desire and know how to call upon thee by diligent prayer.

Father, into thy hands I commend my own and their spirits. Look down from heaven, the habitation of thy holiness and bless them from thy holy hill.

Keep them, oh keep them, unspotted from the world. Grant they may fly youthful lusts, and remember thee, their Creator, in the days of their youth. Train them, I beseech thee, in the way wherein they should go, and when they are old, let them not depart from it.

O thou, who didst sanctify Jeremiah from the womb, and calledst young Samuel betimes, to wear a linen ephod before thee, sanctify their whole spirits, souls and bodies, and preserve them blameless, till the second coming of our Lord Jesus Christ.

O thou, who didst endue Solomon with grace, to choose wisdom before riches and honour, incline their hearts to make the same choice of thee, their only Good. And may they always renounce and triumph over the lust of the flesh, the lust of the eye, and the pride of life.

Finally, do thou, O blessed Jesu, who at twelve years old wast found in the Temple sitting among the doctors, both hearing and asking them questions, grant that these children may love to tread the courts of thy House, and have their ears opened betimes, to receive the discipline of wisdom, that so, if it by thy good pleasure, to prolong the time of their pilgrimage here on earth, they may shine as lights in the world; or, if thou seest it best, to bring down their strength in their journey, and to shorten their days, they may be early fitted by purity of heart, to sing eternal hallelujahs to thee, the Father, and the Holy Ghost, in the Kingdom of Heaven forever.

*Whitefield died September 30, 1770 in the home of Rev.Parsons,
Newburyport, Massachusetts*

[Reprinted from John Gillies, *Memoirs of Rev. George Whitefield*
(New Haven: Horace Mansfield, 1834), facing p.212]

Grant this, O Father, for thy dear Son's sake, Christ Jesus, our Lord. Amen, Amen.

[1] Whitefield, *Sermons on Various Subjects*, 129–132.

Appendix

The conversion of James Gardiner

Among George Whitefield's most cherished friends was Colonel James Gardiner (1688–1745), a Scottish military officer and dragoon who served on the Continent in a number of campaigns. The most notable was his service under John Churchill (1650–1722), the first Duke of Marlborough, at the Battle of Ramillies (1706), where Gardiner was severely wounded. Before his conversion he was known as "the happy rake," and was regarded by his friends as one of the most fortunate men alive during the second decade of the eighteenth century.[1] Tall, stately in his bearing, and gifted with a fine constitution, he had distinguished himself a number of times on the field of battle and seemed destined for a brilliant career. Although he had been raised by a mother who had taken great pains to "instruct him with great tenderness and affection in the principles of true Christianity," Gardiner had long since rejected this childhood instruction.[2] Stationed in Paris during the 1710s as an aide-de-camp to the British ambassador, John Dalrymple (1673–1747), the second Earl of Stair, Gardiner went from one sexual encounter to another in an unbridled pursuit of pleasure. In the words of Philip Doddridge (1702–1751), the Dissenting minister of Northampton who was later his close friend and biographer, "if not the whole business, at least the whole happiness of his life" consisted of these sordid affairs.[3]

This immersion in a lifestyle of sex, seduction and lust, though, was not without some pangs of conscience. On one occasion, when some of his companions were congratulating him on the felicity of his way of life, a dog happened to enter the room in which they were seated, and Gardiner could not help but think to himself, "Oh that I were that dog!"[4] A few spurtive attempts to mend his ways always proved far too weak to resist the force of temptation. But, when he was thirty-one, Gardiner underwent a conversion so striking that Doddridge would later describe it with words such as "astonishing" and "remarkable," "extraordinary" and "amazing."[5]

Towards the middle of July 1719, Gardiner had spent an evening in the company of some friends, the party breaking up around eleven o'clock. Gardiner had a rendezvous with a married woman planned for midnight, and, not wanting to arrive early, he decided to kill the intervening hour by reading. Quite unintentionally, it was a religious book which he picked up to read: *The Christian Soldier; or Heaven taken by storm* (1669) by the Puritan divine Thomas Watson (d. *c.*1686). While he was reading, an unusual blaze of light suddenly fell upon the book, which at first he thought might have been caused by a nearby candle. Lifting up his eyes, though, he saw, to his utter astonishment, a vision of Christ. In the words of Doddridge:

> There was before him, as it were, suspended in the air, a visible representation of the Lord Jesus Christ upon the cross, surrounded on all sides with a glory; and [he] was impressed, as if a voice, or something equivalent to a voice had come to him, to this effect (for he was not confident as to the very words): "Oh sinner! did I suffer this for thee, and are these thy returns?"...Struck with so amazing a phenomenon as this, there remained hardly any life in him; so that he sunk down in the arm-chair in which he sat, and continued, he knew not very exactly how long, insensible.

When he opened his eyes, the vision had gone, but not the impression it had forever made upon his heart and life. He completely forgot his midnight appointment.

> He rose in a tumult of passions not to be conceived, and walked to and fro in his chamber, till he was ready to drop down, in unutterable astonishment and agony of heart, appearing to himself the vilest monster in the creation of God, who had all his lifetime been crucifying Christ afresh by his sins, and now saw, as he assuredly believed, by a miraculous vision, the

horror of what he had done. With this was connected such a view, both of the majesty and goodness of God, as caused him to loathe and abhor himself, to repent as in dust and ashes. He immediately gave judgement against himself, that he was most justly worthy of eternal damnation.[6]

The rest of the night he spent meditating on God's purity and goodness, his spurning of God's grace, and many of the providential escapes from death which he had experienced. His former lifestyle now appeared to him as utterly abhorrent, his sexual addiction was gone, and he was determined to spend the remainder of his time on earth in God's service. Indeed, from this extraordinary conversion till he fell at the Battle of Prestonpans on September 21, 1745, fighting against the Jacobite army of Charles Edward Stuart (1720–1788), his was an "exemplary and truly Christian life."[7]

Though Whitefield made Gardiner's acquaintance only a few years before the latter's death,[8] the evangelist considered the soldier as one of his cherished friends. After his death, Whitefield could say of him: "The late brave Colonel Gardiner was my peculiar Friend."[9] On the other hand, Gardiner was deeply impressed by Whitefield. As he once remarked: "I had rather be that despised persecuted man, to be an instrument in the hand of the Spirit, in converting so many souls, and building up so many in their holy faith, than I would be emperor of the whole world."[10]

1 Philip Doddridge, *Some Remarkable Passages in the Life of the Honourable Col. James Gardiner* §22 [*The Works of the Rev. P. Doddridge, D.D.* (Leeds, 1803), IV, 19]. The complete story of Gardiner's conversion may be found in ibid. §§30–37 (*Works*, IV, 24–29). A brief account of Gardiner's life and conversion may be found in F.W.B. Bullock, *Evangelical Conversion in Great Britain 1696–1845* (St. Leonards on Sea, Sussex: Budd & Gillatt, 1959), 16–21. For a more recent account, see the excellent chapter on Gardiner by Faith Cook in her *Sound of Trumpets* (Edinburgh: Banner of Truth Trust, 1999), 2–17.

2 Doddridge, *Some Remarkable Passages* §9 (*Works*, IV, 11).

3 Ibid. §22 (*Works*, IV, 19).

4 Ibid. §23 (*Works*, IV, 19).

5 Ibid. §§28, 29, 36 (*Works*, IV, 22, 23, 27).

6 Ibid. §33 (*Works*, IV, 25).

7 Ibid. §35 (*Works*, IV, 27).

8 See Letter CCCCLXII to Colonel Gardiner, October 7, 1742 [*The Works of the Reverend George Whitefield, M.A.* (London: Edward and Charles Dilly, 1771), I, 447–448].

9 Letter to General Pepperell, May 28, 1746 [John W. Christie, "Newly Discovered Letters of George Whitefield, 1745-46, II," *Journal of The Presbyterian Historical Society*, 32 (1954), 173]. For Whitefield's letter of condolence to Gardiner's widow, see John W. Christie, "Newly Discovered Letters of George Whitefield, 1745–46, I," *Journal of The Presbyterian Historical Society*, 32 (1954), 82–83.

10 *Some Remarkable Passages* §136 (Works, IV, 89). Gardiner penned these words in a letter he wrote to Philip Doddridge on November 16, 1742, from Ghent, in what was then the Austrian Netherlands.

Endnotes

1   G. Norris Foster, compiled, *First Presbyterian Church (Old South), Newburyport, Massachusetts. Historical Notes and Dates* (n.p., n.d.), 1.

2   *The Baptists in America: A Narrative of the Deputation from the Baptist Union in England to The United States and Canada* (London: T. Ward and Co., 1836), 421–422. For other similar accounts, see L. Tyerman, *The Life of the Rev. George Whitefield* (New York: Anson D.F. Randolph & Co., 1877), II, 602–603, 607. (Henceforth cited as *Life*, II.)

3   Foster, *First Presbyterian Church (Old South)*, 1, 8. Tyerman gives the date for the bone's return as 1837 (*George Whitefield*, II, 606). Robert Philip, Whitefield's nineteenth-century biographer, knew the thief and urged him to return it. The thief sought to show Philip the bone in 1835, but the latter refused to gaze upon it. See Philip's *The Life and Times of the Reverend George Whitefield, M.A.* (London: George Virtue, 1838), 550–551.

4   "Charles Wesley in 1739 by Joseph Williams of Kidderminster," introd. Geoffrey F. Nuttall, *Proceedings of the Wesley Historical Society*, 42, No. 6 (December 1980), 182. On Williams, see Geoffrey F. Nuttall, "Methodism and the Older Dissent: Some Perspectives," *The Journal of the United Reformed Church History Society* 2 (1978–1982), 261–264.

5   Cited Willard Connely, *The True Chesterfield: Manners—Women—Education* (London: Cassell and Co. Ltd., 1939), 179. On Bolingbroke's profession of Deism, see Philip Dormer Stanhope, *Characters* (1778 ed.; repr. Los Angeles: William Andrews Clark Memorial Library, University of California, 1990), 22.

6   "To the Reader," the Preface to Joseph Smith, *The Character, Preaching, etc. of the Reverend Mr. George Whitefield.*

Impartially Represented and Supported in George Whitefield, *Fifteen Sermons Preached on Various Important Subjects* (London, 1792), 5–6.

[7] "A Concise Character of the Late Rev. Mr. Whitefield," *The Works of Augustus Toplady, B.A.* (London: J. Chidley, 1837), 494.

[8] "George Whitefield: A Critical Essay" in *George Whitefield's Journals (1737–1741)* (1905 ed.; repr. Gainesville, Florida: Scholars' Facsimiles & Reprints, 1969), 15. On the comparison of Whitefield with the mediæval reformer John Wycliffe (*c.*1330–1384), see also Gordon Rupp, *Religion in England 1688–1791* (Oxford: Clarendon Press, 1986), 339.

[9] The best biographical study of Whitefield is Arnold Dallimore, *George Whitefield: The Life and Times of the Great Evangelist of the Eighteenth-Century Revival* (1970 and 1979 eds.; repr. Westchester, Illinois: Cornerstone Books, 1979 and 1980), 2 vols. Dallimore has also written a one-volume account of Whitefield's life: *George Whitefield: Evangelist of the 18th–Century Revival* (London: The Wakeman Trust, 1990). For a shorter study of Whitefield, see John H. Armstrong, "George Whitefield 1714–1770" in his *Five Great Evangelists* (Fearn, Ross-shire: Christian Focus Publications, 1997), 15–70. For two studies that are more critical and controversial in nature, see Harry S. Stout, *The Divine Dramatist: George Whitefield and the Rise of Modern Evangelicalism* (Grand Rapids: William B. Eerdmans Publ. Co., 1991) and Frank Lambert, *"Pedlar in Divinity"* in *George Whitefield and the Transatlantic Revivals, 1737–1770* (Princeton: Princeton University Press, 1994). For an insightful critique of Stout, see Eric Carlsson, "Book Reviews: Harry S. Stout, *The Divine Dramatist: George Whitefield and the Rise of Modern Evangelicalism,*" *Trinity Journal*, NS, 14, No. 2 (Fall 1993), 238–247.

[10] On the role that reading played in his conversion and his subsequent growth as a Christian, see Lambert, *"Pedlar in Divinity"*, 17–21. It is interesting that it was Christian litera-

regarded as the beginning of the evangelical movement" [http://www.spartacus.schoolnet.co.uk/REevangelical.htm; accessed January 1, 2000]. Gordon Wakefield, though, in his essay "John and Charles Wesley: A Tale of Two Brothers," has it right when he says that it was Whitefield "and not the Wesleys who may be said to have begun the Evangelical Revival in 1737" [Geoffrey Rowell, ed., *The English Religious Tradition and the Genius of Anglicanism* (Nashville: Abingdon Press, 1992), 172].

27 For instance, on September 26, 1740, in Boston.

28 In light of his own itinerant ministry, it is interesting to read the following remarks on Jesus' ministry. Christ, he wrote in 1756, "taught all that were willing to hear, on a mount, in a ship, or by the sea-side" [Letter MCXVII to the Bishop of B—, February 2, 1756 (*The Works of the Reverend George Whitefield, M.A.* [London: Edward and Charles Dilly, 1771], III, 157)]. (Henceforth cited as *Works*, III).

29 *Works*, III, 379, 387.

30 *Jacob's Ladder* (*Sermons on Important Subjects*, 774).

31 Iain Murray, "Introduction" to *George Whitefield's Journals*, 13.

32 George Whitefield, Letter to Daniel Abbot, February 24, 1739 [Graham C.G. Thomas, "George Whitefield and Friends: The Correspondence of Some Early Methodists," *The National Library of Wales Journal*, 27 (1991), 83].

33 Cited Dallimore, *George Whitefield*, I, 263–264.

34 Cited ibid., I, 268.

35 Augustus Montague Toplady, "Anecdotes, Incidents and Historic Passages" in his *Works*, 495; John Gillies, *Memoirs of Rev. George Whitefield* (New Haven: Horace Mansfield, 1834), 284.

36 Dallimore, *George Whitefield*, II, 522.

37 For the numbers, see Dallimore, *George Whitefield*, I, 263, 267, 295–296; II, 522–523.

38 On his ministry in Wales, see especially S.M. Houghton, "George Whitefield and Welsh Methodism," *The Evangelical*

Quarterly, 22 (1950), 276–289; Eifion Evans, "Priorities in Revival: George Whitefield and the Revival in Wales" in his *Fire in the Thatch. The True Nature of Religious Revival* (Bryntirion, Bridgend, Mid Glamorgan: Evangelical Press of Wales, 1996), 84–102; George E. Clarkson, *George Whitefield and Welsh Calvinistic Methodism* (Lewiston, New York: Edwin Mellen Press, 1996). On his preaching ministry in Scotland, see D. Butler, *John Wesley and George Whitefield in Scotland, or, The Influence of the Oxford Methodists on Scottish Religion* (Edinburgh/London: William Blackwood and Sons, 1898), 4–66.

39 He was in America during 1738, 1739–1741, 1744–1748, 1751–1752, 1754–1755, 1763–1765 and 1769–1770.

40 See the informing discussion of travel in this period and the following century by Sven Birkerts, *The Gutenberg Elegies: The Fate of Reading in an Electronic Age* (New York: Fawcett Columbine, 1994), 24–25.

41 Harry S. Stout, "Heavenly Comet," *Christian History*, 38 (1993), 13.

42 Ibid., 13–14.

43 See pp.40–49.

44 *The Journal of the Rev. John Wesley, A.M.*, ed. Nehemiah Curnock (1911 ed.; repr. London: The Epworth Press, 1960), II, 256–257, n.1.

45 See Michael A.G. Haykin, *Revivals and Signs and Wonders: Some Evangelical Perspectives from the Eighteenth Century* (Richmond Hill, Ontario: Canadian Christian Publications, 1994), 17–29.

46 C.C. Goen, *Revivalism and Separatism in New England, 1740–1800. Strict Congregationalists and Separate Baptists in the Great Awakening* (1962 ed.; repr. Middletown, Connecticut: Wesleyan University Press, 1987), 240.

47 Letter to Thomas Foxcroft, May 24, 1740 [Thomas Foxcroft Correspondence, Firestone Library, Princeton University, cited Milton J. Coalter, Jr., "The Life of Gilbert Tennent: A Case Study of Continental Pietism's Influence on

the First Great Awakening in the Middle Colonies" (Unpublished Ph.D. dissertation, Princeton University, 1982), 151]. On Dickinson's concerns about Whitefield, see also Bryan F. Le Beau, *Jonathan Dickinson and the Formative Years of American Presbyterianism* (Lexington, Kentucky: The University Press of Kentucky, 1997), 117–118.

48 See pp.178–179. See also Dallimore, *George Whitefield*, II, 519–520; Rupp, *Religion in England*, 377–388.

49 These are the words of Thomas Prince (1687–1758), a New England pastor and historian [cited John Gillies, *Historical Collections of the Accounts of Revival* (1845 ed.; repr. Edinburgh: The Banner of Truth Trust, 1981), 350, 351].

50 Stout, "Heavenly Comet," 13.

51 David Hume (1711–1776), a Scottish philosopher, was a vehement critic of Christianity.

52 David Garrick (1717–1779) was widely regarded as the greatest British actor of the day.

53 Repr. *The Banner of Truth*, 79 (April 1970), 25–26.

54 "George Whitefield: Man Alive. A Review Article," *Crux*, 16, No.4 (December 1980), 26.

55 Letter DCCXIX to Dr. D—, December 21, 1748 (*Works*, II, 216).

56 *On the Death of the Rev. George Whitefield. 1770* in *The Poems of Phillis Wheatley*, ed. Julian D. Mason, Jr. (Rev. ed.; Chapel Hill/London: The University of North Carolina Press, 1989), 56. For a brief overview of Wheatley's life, see ibid., 2–13. See also Jeanne Knepper and Will Gravely, "Wheatley, Phillis" in Donald M. Lewis, ed., *The Blackwell Dictionary of Evangelical Biography 1730–1860* (Oxford/ Cambridge, Massachusetts: Blackwell Publishers, 1995), II, 1177.

57 Geoffrey F. Nuttall, "George Whitefield: A Commemorative Address," *Churchman* 108 (1994), 321–322. See also Dallimore, *George Whitefield: Evangelist of the 18th-Century Revival*, 221–222.

58 *The Life and Times of the Reverend George Whitefield, A.M.,*

565.

59 Helpful in the following study of Whitefield's spirituality have been James M. Gordon, *Evangelical Spirituality* (London: SPCK, 1991), 53–66 and Packer, "The Spirit with the Word", 166–189.

60 "'Methodism' and the origins of English-Speaking Evangelicalism" in Mark A. Noll, David W. Bebbingion, and George A. Rawlyk, eds., *Evangelicalism: Comparative Studies of Popular Protestantism in North America, the British Isles, and Beyond, 1700–1990* (New York/Oxford: Oxford University Press, 1994), 20–21.

61 Benjamin Keach, *Gospel Mysteries Unveiled* (1701 ed.; repr. London: L.I. Higham, 1817), III, 310.

62 On these societies, see especially A.G. Craig, "The Movement for Reformation of Manners" (Unpublished Ph. D. Thesis, University of Edinburgh, 1980); Craig Rose, "Providence, Protestant Union and Godly Reformation in the 1690s," *Transactions of the Royal Historical Society*, 6th. Series, III (1993), 151–169 and the literature cited in ibid., 151, n. 1.

63 J.H. Plumb, *The First Four Georges* (London: B.T. Batsford Ltd., 1956), 39–42.

64 J.H. Plumb, *Sir Robert Walpole* (Clifton, New Jersey: Augustus M. Kelley, 1973), II, 114.

65 Ibid., II, 114.

66 Roy Porter, *English Society in the Eighteenth Century* (Harmondsworth, Middlesex: Penguin Books Ltd., 1982), 279.

67 Selina Hastings, "A peeress with a passion for piety," *Sunday Telegraph* (December 14, 1997).

68 See pp.28–29.

69 Letter CIX to Mr. Thomas Periam, November 10, 1739 (*Works*, I, 104). See also Whitefield's remark regarding a Mrs. Palmer, who was converted under his ministry in New England: "I should think myself well rewarded had our Lord made me instrumental of turning only Dear Mrs. Palmer

from a life of polite civility to real & undissembled godliness" [Letter to Isaac Royal, May 21, 1746 in John W. Christie, "Newly Discovered Letters of George Whitefield, 1745–46, II," *Journal of The Presbyterian Historical Society*, 32 (1954), 169]. This second installment of a three-part article will henceforth be cited as Christie, "Newly Discovered Letters II."

70 See pp.191–192.

71 Letter CCCXI to Serjeant B—, July 25, 1741 (*Works*, I, 284).

72 See also George Whitefield, Letter MCCCLX, July 21, 1767 (*Works*, III, 349–350).

73 Cited Tyerman, *Life*, II, 242.

74 *Some Remarks on a Pamphlet, entitled, The Enthusiasm of Methodists and Papists compar'd* (London: W. Strahan, 1749), 30. The allusion is to the riot in Ephesus over the threat that Christianity posed to the worship of the goddess Artemis or Diana (Acts 19:21–40).

75 *Sermons on Important Subjects*, 544. In this particular volume this sermon has the title *On Regeneration*. When it was first published in 1737, it had the title given in the text. For a recent edition of the 1737 version of this sermon, see Timothy L. Smith, *Whitefield & Wesley on the New Birth* (Grand Rapids: Francis Asbury Press of Zondervan Publishing House, 1986), 65–78. See also Smith's commentary on this sermon, ibid., 63–65.

76 *Sermons on Important Subjects*, 544.

77 Ibid., 545.

78 Letter CCCVIII to Mr. I— F—, July 24, 1741 (*Works*, I, 281).

79 The full sermon can be found in *Sermons on Important Subjects*, 500–511. For a modern edition, see Smith, *Whitefield & Wesley on the New Birth*, 123–137.

80 Smith, *Whitefield & Wesley on the New Birth*, 121.

81 *Sermons on Important Subjects*, 500–502.

82 See p.143.

83 *Sermons on Important Subjects*, 502.

84 Letter to Jonathan Thompson, May 11, 1746 (Christie, "Newly Discovered Letters II," 161). See also *Jacob's Ladder* (*Sermons on Important Subjects*, 772–773): "You need not be afraid of our destroying inward holiness, by preaching the doctrine of the imputation of Christ's righteousness, that one is the foundation, the other, the superstructure; to talk of my having the righteousness of Christ imputed to my soul, without my having the holiness of Christ imparted to it, and bringing forth the fruits of the Spirit as an evidence of it, is only deceiving ourselves."

85 *Sermons on Important Subjects*, 502. Italics added.

86 Ibid., 502–503.

87 John Keegan, *The Face of Battle* (London: Jonathan Cape, 1976), 183–184.

88 See p.202.

89 Letter to John Sims, November 30, 1745 [John W. Christie, "Newly Discovered Letters of George Whitefield, 1745–46, I," *Journal of The Presbyterian Historical Society*, 32 (1954), 73]. See also his Letter to Mr. Straham, June 16, 1746 [John W. Christie, "Newly Discovered Letters of George Whitefield, 1745–46, III," *Journal of The Presbyterian Historical Society*, 32 (1954), 257]: Christ is "the Believer's Asylum. He is the Believer's all in all. I find Him to be so dayly [*sic*]. Having nothing, in Him I possess all things." The first installment of this article is henceforth cited as Christie, "Newly Discovered Letters I" and the third installment as Christie, "Newly Discovered Letters III."

90 Letter MCXC to Lady G— H—, December 15, 1757 (*Works*, III, 225).

91 Earlier versions of portions of this section appeared as Michael A.G. Haykin, "Defenders of the faith: George Whitefield and the nature of Christian perfection," *Evangelical Times*, 32, No. 10 (October 1998), 23; idem, "Evangelical piety: grounded in justification by faith alone," *Evangelical Times*, 34, No. 1 (January 2000), 14; idem,

"Christ, our wisdom and our righteousness," *Evangelical Times*, 34, No. 2 (February 2000), 14. Used by permission.

[92] Timothy L. Smith, "George Whitefield and Wesleyan Perfectionism," *The Wesleyan Theological Journal*, 19, No. 1 (Spring 1984), 74–75.

[93] See p.132.

[94] *Sermons on Important Subjects*, 505.

[95] Ibid., 193.

[96] Letter to Herbert Jenkins, May 12, 1746 (Christie, "Newly Discovered Letters II," 162–163).

[97] Letter to Gabriel Harris, May 2, 1746 (Christie, "Newly Discovered Letters I," 87).

[98] Letter to Howel Harris, May 2, 1746 (Christie, "Newly Discovered Letters I," 88); Letter to Mr. Kennedy, May 2, 1746 (Christie, "Newly Discovered Letters I," 89); Letter to Herbert Jenkins, May 12, 1746 (Christie, "Newly Discovered Letters II," 162–163).

[99] Letter to Elizabeth Longden, May 2, 1746 (Christie, "Newly Discovered Letters I," 86). Elizabeth Longden was Whitefield's mother, who, six years after the death of her first husband, married Capel Longden, in 1722. It was not a happy marriage. See Dallimore, *George Whitefield*, I, 52–55. On William Cudworth and his views, see Peter L. Lineham, "Cudworth, William" in Lewis, ed., *The Blackwell Dictionary of Evangelical Biography*, I, 278–279.

[100] Letter CCLXII to Mrs. S—, February 17, 1741 (*Works*, I, 245).

[101] Letter MCXII to Lady Huntingdon, December 31, 1755 (*Works*, III, 153).

[102] Letter CCCXCV to Mr. B—, February 5, 1742 (*Works*, I, 366–367).

[103] For different perspectives on this controversy between Whitefield and the Wesleys, see Iain Murray, "Prefatory Note" to George Whitefield, *A Letter to the Rev. Mr. John Wesley in Answer to His Sermon entitled "Free Grace"* (*George Whitefield's Journals*, 564–568); Frank Baker, "Whitefield's

Break with the Wesleys," *The Church Quarterly*, 3, No. 2 (October 1970), 103–113; Dallimore, *George Whitefield*, II, passim; Smith, "George Whitefield and Wesleyan Perfectionism," 63–85; J. D. Walsh, "Wesley vs. Whitefield," *Christian History*, 38 (1993), 34–37; Clarkson, *George Whitefield and Welsh Calvinistic Methodism*, 33–47.

104 J.I. Packer, "Steps to the Renewal of the Christian People" in *Serving the People of God [The Collected Shorter Writings of J.I. Packer*, vol. 2, (Carlisle, Cumbria: Paternoster Press, 1998), 74].

105 On one occasion Howel Harris told Wesley: "You grieve God's people by your opposition to electing love" (cited Clarkson, *George Whitefield and Welsh Calvinistic Methodism*, 78).

106 Letter to Robert Carr Brackenbury, September 15, 1790 [*The Letters of the Rev. John Welsey, A.M.*, ed. John Telford (1931 ed.; repr. London: The Epworth Press, 1960), VIII, 238].

107 W.E. Sangster, *The Path to Perfection. An Examination and Restatement of John Wesley's Doctrine of Christian Perfection* (London: Hodder and Stoughton, 1943), 25; John R. Tyson, *Charles Wesley on Sanctification. A Biographical and Theological Study* (Grand Rapids: Francis Asbury Press of Zondervan Publishing House, 1986), 227–301. Further examination of this aspect of Wesley's thought may be found in Harald Lindström, *Wesley and Sanctification: A Study in the Doctrine of Salvation* (Stockholm: Nya Bokförlags Aktiebolaget, 1946).

108 *A Plain Account of Christian Perfection* (1777) [*The Works of the Rev. John Wesley, A.M.* (London: John Mason, 1830), XI, 396].

109 Ibid. (*Works*, XI, 402); Letter to Sarah Rutter, December 5, 1789 (*Letters*, VIII, 190).

110 Letter to Mrs. Anne Dutton (June 25, 1740?) [*The Works of John Wesley*, ed. Frank Baker (Oxford: Clarendon Press, 1982), 26:15]. See also the remarks on Wesley's inconsistency at this point by Jeffrey, "Introduction" to his ed., *A Burning and a Shining Light*, 32–33.

111 John A. Newton, "Perfection and Spirituality in the Methodist Tradition," *The Church Quarterly*, 3, No. 2 (October 1970), 102.

112 Letter to a Friend in London, April 25, 1741 [*Letters of George Whitefield for the Period 1734–1742* (Edinburgh: The Banner of Truth Trust, 1976)]. This book is a reprint of the first volume of the *Works* of Whitefield along with 34 addditional letters. This work is henceforth cited as *Letters*.

113 "John and Charles Wesley," 191.

114 In 1753 he could similarly declare: "I can truly say, that for these many years last past, no sin hath had dominion over me" [Letter DCCCCLXXV to Mr. S—, May 27, 1753 (*Works*, III, 14)].

115 Letter CLXIX to the Rev. John Wesley, March 26, 1740 (*Works*, I, 155–156).

116 Letter CCXIX to Mr. Accourt, September 23, 1740 (*Works*, I, 209).

117 Letter CCXXI to the Rev. John Wesley, September 25, 1740 (*Works*, I, 210–212).

118 See Dallimore, *George Whitefield*, II, 563.

119 Cited Frank Baker, *William Grimshaw 1708–1763* (London: Epworth Press, 1963), 73–74. Grimshaw predeceased both John and his brother Charles, and thus never became the leader of the Methodists. Tyson wrongly attributes this letter to Charles Wesley (*Charles Wesley on Sanctification*, 301).

120 *Some Remarks on a Pamphlet*, 26.

121 On the Erskines, see Alan P.F. Sell, "The Message of the Erskines for Today," *The Evangelical Quarterly*, 60 (1988), 299–316; Joel Beeke, "The Ministry of the Erskines" (Two papers presented at the 21st Annual Banner of Truth Ministers' Conference, Grantham, Pennsylvania, May 26–27, 1999). For another perspective on Whitefield's relationship with the Erskines, see also Kenneth B.E. Roxburgh, *Thomas Gillespie and the Origins of the Relief Church in 18th Century Scotland* (Bern: Peter Lang, 1999), 31–39.

122 Letter 33 to John Willison, August 17, 1742 (*Letters*, 514–515).

123 Letter CCCXXXIX to Thomas Noble, August 8, 1741 (*Works*, I, 308).

124 Letter CCCXLIII, August 11, 1741 (*Works*, I, 311).

125 Letter CCCLVI, October 2, 1741 (*Works*, I, 323).

126 Letter to Rev'd. Mr. Gee, June 21, 1746 (Christie, "Newly Discovered Letters III," 261). Compare his following remarks: Letter to John Harvey Sweetland, February 21, 1738: "I wish I had 1000 lives that I might offer them all for God, for indeed…he is worthy of them all" [Graham C.G. Thomas, "George Whitefield and Friends: The Correspondence of Some Early Methodists," *The National Library of Wales Journal*, 26 (1990), 387–388]; Letter DCCC-CLXXI to Mr. G—, April 17, 1753 (*Works*, III, 9–10): "Was it not sinful, I could wish for a thousand hands, a thousand tongues, and a thousand lives: all should be employed night and day, without ceasing, in promoting the glory of the ever-lovely, ever-loving Jesus."

127 Letter [DCCCCLXXXV] to Mr. G—, July 21, 1753 (*Works*, III, 24).

128 Letter DLXXXVIII to Mr. B—, May 8, 1747 (*Works*, II, 96–97).

129 Letter to Mr. Adams, May 15, 1746 (Christie, "Newly Discovered Letters II," 163).

130 Letter MCXLII to Mrs. C—, June 21, 1756 (*Works*, III, 185).

131 Letter MCLXIV to the Reverend Mr. B—, March 10, 1757 (*Works*, III, 202).

132 Letter MCCCLXXXIX to the Reverend Mr. T—, July 4, 1768 (*Works*, III, 371).

133 For a study of this subject, see the insightful article by D. Bruce Hindmarsh, " 'My chains fell off, my heart was free': Early Methodist Conversion Narrative in England," *Church History*, 68 (1999), 910–929.

134 The following account of Olivers' conversion comes

from Thomas Jackson, ed., *Wesley's Veterans. Lives of Early Methodist Preachers Told by Themselves* (1837–1838 ed.; repr. London: Robert Culley, 1909), I, 205–206.

135 On the life of Robinson, see especially Graham W. Hughes, *With Freedom Fired. The Story of Robert Robinson Cambridge Nonconformist* (London: Carey Kingsgate Press, 1955); L.G. Champion, "Robert Robinson: A Pastor In Cambridge," *The Baptist Quarterly*, 31 (1985–1986), 241–246; Len Addicott, "Introduction" to L.G. Champion, and K.A.C. Parsons, *Church Book: St Andrew's Street Baptist Church, Cambridge 1720–1832* (London: Baptist Historical Society, 1991), viii–xviii. I am well aware that Robinson's theological convictions in his final days have been the subject of considerable discussion and disagreement. There are reports that he questioned the doctrine of the Trinity, for instance. However, on the other hand, one of his oldest friends, Coxe Feary (1759–1822) pastor of the Calvinistic Baptist work in Bluntisham, Huntingdonshire, recorded a conversation that he had with Robinson but a month before the latter's death in 1790. Robinson affirmed that when it came to the doctrine of the Trinity he was neither a Unitarian nor an Arian. "My soul rests its whole hope of salvation," he solemnly told Feary, "on the atonement of Jesus Christ, my Lord and my God."[Joseph Belcher, "Note *" in his ed., *The Complete Works of the Rev. Andrew Fuller* (Repr. Harrisonburg, Virginia: Sprinkle Publications, 1988), II, 223–224].

136 Andrew Fuller, "Anecdote," *The Evangelical Magazine*, 2 (1794), 72–73. Fuller had received this account of Robinson's conversion from Robinson himself. The story was written under the name of "Gaius," the pen-name that Fuller regularly used.

137 Letter to George Whitefield, 10 May 1758 [William Robinson, ed., *Select Works of the Rev. Robert Robinson, of Cambridge* (London: J. Heaton & Son, 1861), 166–167].

138 Fuller, "Anecdote," 73.

139 Letter to George Whitefield, 10 May 1758 (Robinson,

ed., *Select Works*, 167); William Robinson, "Memoir [of Robert Robinson]" in his ed., *Select Works*, xv–xvi, footnote.

140 On this hymn, see the remarks of Erik Routley, *I'll Praise My Maker. A study of the hymns of certain authors who stand in or near the tradition of English Calvinism 1700–1850* (London: Independent Press Ltd., 1951), 260–262.

141 *An Account of the Life, Ministry, and Writings of the Late Rev. John Fawcett, D.D.* (London: Baldwin, Cradock, and Joy, 1818), 15–16.

142 Letter to Jonathan Thompson, May 11, 1746 (Christie, "Newly Discovered Letters II," 161).

143 Letter to John Redman, May 28, 1746 (Christie, "Newly Discovered Letters II," 174–175).

144 Letter DCX to Mr. A—, August 27, 1747 (*Works*, II, 117).

145 Letter to William Pepperell, May 28, 1746 (Christie, "Newly Discovered Letters II," 172). As he wrote three years later: "Like a pure chrystal [*sic*], I would transmit all the glory he is pleased to pour upon me, and never claim as my own, what is his sole property" [Letter DCCXXXVI to Lady G—, February 22, 1749 (*Works*, II, 234)].

146 Letter LXI, August 7, 1739 (*Works*, I, 60).

147 Letter XXIX, December 23, 1737 (*Works*, I, 32).

148 Letter CCLXXVIII to Mr. S—, May 5, 1741 (*Works*, I, 261).

149 Letter MCII to Lady Huntingdon, September 24, 1755 (*Works*, III, 144).

150 Witness a letter he wrote while in Lisbon in the spring of 1754. He thanked God "for the great wonder of the reformation" and "also for that glorious deliverance wrought out for us a few years past." The latter is a reference to the defeat of Charles Edward Stuart (1720–1788), also known as the Young Pretender or Bonnie Prince Charlie, at the Battle of Culloden (1746). The prince had attempted to overthrow the Protestant George II and restore the Roman Catholic dynasty of the Stuarts to the throne of England [Letter

MXXXVI to Mr.—, April 3, 1754 (*Works*, III, 79)].

[151] Letter MCVIII to the Honourable A— O—, November 8, 1755 (*Works*, III, 149). For similar sentiments, see also his Letter MCV to Mr. B—, November 1, 1755 (*Works*, III, 146–147).

[152] Letter DCXCVIII to the Reverend Mr. E—, October 12, 1748 (*Works*, II, 193). See also Letter CCCCLXI to Edmund Jones, October 6, 1742 (*Works*, I, 446): "I care not if the name of George Whitefield be banished out of the world, so that Jesus be exalted in it. Glory be to his great name…" For further examples, see Dallimore, *George Whitefield*, II, 518–519.

[153] Letter CCCCXCIX to Mr. R—, December 24, 1742 (*Works*, II, 4–5). Two years earlier he put the same point this way: "because Jesus Christ hath shewn such mercy to me, I desire that all others should be made as happy, nay happier than I am myself" [Letter CLXXXIII to the Allegheny Indians, May 21, 1740 (*Works*, I, 174)].

[154] Gilbert Thomas, *William Cowper and the Eighteenth Century* (London: Ivor Nicholson and Watson, 1935), 180; Stuart C. Henry, *George Whitefield: Wayfaring Witness* (New York: Abingdon Press, 1957), 95–114.

[155] "Preparation: the Power of Whitefield's Ministry," 23. For a similar judgement, see Packer, "The Spirit and the Word," 188–189.

[156] Murrary, "Prefatory Note," 564.

[157] Letter CVI to John Hutton, November 10, 1739 (*Works*, I, 101).

[158] Letter CXIII to the Rev. Mr. S—, November 10, 1739 (*Works*, I, 108).

[159] Letter CCCCLVI to Mr. F—, September 22, 1742 (*Works*, I, 439). In this letter he mentions being impressed by John Calvin's meekness when he refused to respond in kind to Luther's attack on those who shared Calvin's Reformed theology, namely the Zürich theologians. On this incident, see T.H.L. Parker, *Portrait of Calvin* (London: SCM Press

Ltd., 1954), 110–112. Earlier Whitefield said that he had read nothing by Calvin [Letter to John Wesley, August 25, 1740 (*Works*, I, 205)]. Obviously in the two years between this letter to Wesley and that of 1742 he had read something of the life of Calvin. Yet, he could still affirm that he embraced Calvinism "not because Calvin, but Jesus Christ...has taught it to me" [Letter to Benjamin Colman, September 24, 1742 (*Works*, I, 442)].

160 *Some Remarks on a Pamphlet*, 43–44.

161 Letter 33 to John Willison, August 17, 1742 (*Letters*, 515).

162 Letter MMCCLXXX to Mr. S—, March 13, 1763 (*Works*, III, 288). For the same description of the Puritans, see also *The Seed of the Woman, and the Seed of the Serpent* (*Sermons on Important Subjects*, 44); *Spiritual Baptism* (*Sermons on Important Subjects*, 730); *Observations on Some Fatal Mistakes* (3rd ed.; London, 1763), 21.

163 Letter MCCCV to Mr. S— S—, March 10, 1764 (*Works*, III, 307).

164 *Observations on Some Fatal Mistakes*, 21–22.

165 "Recommendatory Preface" in *The Works of that eminent servant of Christ, John Bunyan* (Philadelphia: John Ball, 1850), I, v. This passage can also be found in Tyerman, *George Whitefield*, II, 508.

166 Lambert, *"Pedlar in Divinity,"* 145.

167 Ibid., 142–146.

168 Letter DCCXI to the Rev. Mr. L.—, November 19, 1748 (*Works*, II, 206); Letter CXXXVIII to Ralph Erskine (*Works*, I, 128–129). Whitefield told Erskine that Boston's book had "under God been of much service to my soul." For another reference to Boston, see *The Seed of the Woman, and the Seed of the Serpent* (*Sermons on Important Subjects*, 42), where he calls Boston "an excellent Scots divine."

169 "Recommendatory Preface" (*Works of...John Bunyan*, I, v). For another reference to Goodwin, see *Marks of a True Conversion* (*Sermons on Important Subjects*, 274).

170 Letter DCCLXXXIX to Mr. L—, December 3, 1749

(*Works*, II, 295).

171 Dallimore, *George Whitefield*, II, 481.

172 Ibid., II, 493; *Walking with God* (*Sermons on Important Subjects*, 48); *Observations on Some Fatal Mistakes*, 21.

173 Letter to John Wesley, August 9, 1740 (in Dallimore, *George Whitefield*, II, 564); Letter DCCXI to the Rev. Mr. L.—, November 19, 1748 (*Works*, II, 206). Also see Dallimore, *George Whitefield*, I, 144; *Marks of a True Conversion* (*Sermons on Important Subjects*, 274).

174 *Observations on Some Fatal Mistakes*, 21.

175 *The Lord our Righteousness* (*Sermons on Important Subjects*, 193); *The Good Shepherd—A Farewell Sermon* (*Sermons on Important Subjects*, 782).

176 Dallimore, *George Whitefield*, II, 564.

177 Letter MCXIX to the Bishop of B—, February 16, 1756 (*Works*, III, 163).

178 Packer, "The Spirit with the Word," 174. On Whitefield's use of Henry, see David Crump, "The Preaching of George Whitefield and His Use of Matthew Henrys' *Commentary*," *Crux*, 25, No. 3 (September 1989), 19–28. Crump demonstrates that while "Henry's *Commentary* played a significant role in shaping Whitefield's understanding of the passages upon which he preached," the evangelist was "no slavish plagiarizer of Henry." His use of the Puritan *Commentary* was "as he deemed it helpful throughout his preaching career" (ibid., 23). From this study Crump generalizes: "Henry's indepth, practical, Calvinistic and biblical exposition served as the educational backdrop for almost every one of Whitefield's sermons" (ibid., 24).

179 *The Temptation of Christ* (*Sermons on Important Subjects*, 220)

180 "Preaching of George Whitefield," 24. For Whitefield's appreciation of Baxter's pastoral labours, see Letter DXLIV to Mr. J— S—, December 31, 1743 (*Works*, II, 47–48).

181 "John Calvin and George Whitefield" in *Able Ministers of the New Testament* (London: The Puritan and Reformed

Studies Conference, 1964), 95. Clarkson fails to develop Whitefield's indebtedness to the Puritans in his discussion of the evangelist's Calvinism, *George Whitefield and Welsh Calvinistic Methodism*, 21–32.

182 Murray, "Prefatory Note," 564; Dallimore, *George Whitefield*, I, 404–405; Packer, "The Spirit with the Word," 178–179.

183 *The Beloved of God* (*Sermons on Important Subjects*, 680). See also Dallimore, *George Whitefield*, I, 406.

184 Letter C, November 10, 1739 (*Works*, I, 95).

185 Dallimore, *George Whitefield*, I, 405–406.

186 Letter XCIV to the Rev. Mr. P—, November 10, 1739 (*Works*, I, 90).

187 Letter LXXXII, November 10, 1739 (*Works*, I, 79).

188 Letter to Samuel Church, May 11, 1746 (Christie, "Newly Discovered Letters II," 160).

189 Letter XCIV to the Rev. Mr. P—, November 10, 1739 (*Works*, I, 89).

190 "The Spiritual Travels of Nathan Cole" in Richard L. Bushman, ed., *The Great Awakening: Documents on the Revival of Religion, 1740–1745* (1970 ed.; repr. Chapel Hill/London: University of North Carolina Press for the Institute of Early American History and Culture, 1989), 68.

191 Ibid., 71.

192 Letter DCXV to Mrs. S—, September 6, 1747 (*Works*, II, 120).

193 *Pace* Harry S. Stout, "George Whitefield in Three Countries" in Mark A. Noll, David W. Bebbington and George A. Rawlyk, eds., *Evangelicalism: Comparative Studies of Popular Protestantism in North America, the British Isles, and Beyond, 1700–1900* (New York/Oxford: Oxford University Press, 1994), 68–69.

194 See, for example, his *Journals*, 541.

195 "Great George," *Christianity Today*, 30, No. 13 (September 19, 1986), 12.

Select bibliography

John H. Armstrong, "George Whitefield 1714–1770" in his *Five Great Evangelists* (Fearn, Ross-shire: Christian Focus Publications, 1997), 15–70.

Christian History, 38 (1993) [this entire issue is devoted to Whitefield].

David Crump, "The Preaching of George Whitefield and His Use of Matthew Henry's *Commentary*," *Crux*, 25, No. 3 (September 1989), 19–28.

Arnold Dallimore, *George Whitefield: The Life and Times of the Great Evangelist of the Eighteenth-Century Revival*, 2 vols. (1970 and 1979 eds.; repr. Westchester, Illinois: Cornerstone Books, 1979 and 1980).

John Lewis Gilmore, "Preparation: the Power of Whitefield's Ministry," *Christianity Today*, 24, No. 5 (March 7, 1980), 22–24.

James M. Gordon, *Evangelical Spirituality* (London: SPCK, 1991), 53–66.

Stuart C. Henry, *George Whitefield: Wayfaring Witness* (New York: Abingdon Press, 1957).

J.I. Packer, "George Whitefield: Man Alive. A Review Article," *Crux*, 16, No. 4 (December 1980), 23–26.

J.I. Packer, "The Spirit with the Word: The Reformational Revivalism of George Whitefield" in W.P. Stephens, ed., *The Bible, the Reformation and the Church. Essays in Honour of James Atkinson (Journal for the Study of the New Testament Supplement Series*, 105; Sheffield: Sheffield Academic

Press, 1995), 166–189.

L. Tyerman, *The Life of the Rev. George Whitefield* (New York: Anson D.F. Randolph & Co., 1877), 2 vols.

George Whitefield, *Sermons on Important Subjects* (London: Thomas Tegg, 1833).

The Works of the Reverend George Whitefield, M.A. (London: Edward and Charles Dilly, 1771), 6 vols.

George Whitefield's Journals (London: The Banner of Truth Trust, 1960).

Reading
spiritual classics

In recent days, "spirituality" has become something
of a buzzword in Reformed circles. This is all well
and good. But there is a downside to the story. The
spiritual books being read are invariably drawn from
streams that are seriously deficient when it comes to
the truths Reformed believers delight in. This series
has been designed to partially fill this gap by provid-
ing choice selections from various Reformed writers. As publishers we are convinced, as John Benton
has recently stated, that while God is deeply con-
cerned about the sin of the world, he is "more con-
cerned about the spirituality of the church."

Now, the reading of spiritual classics should differ from other types of reading. Whereas one reads
a newspaper, dictionary or textbook for factual
information or immediate answers to queries, in
spiritual reading one seeks to inflame the heart as
well as inform the mind. Spiritual reading, as
Eugene Peterson has noted, should therefore be
"leisurely, repetitive, reflective reading." It should
not be hurried, for attention needs to be paid to
what the Spirit of God is saying through the text.
And texts rich in spiritual nourishment beg to be re-
read again and again so that their truth and beauty

might be savoured.

Of course, when it comes to spiritual classics, the Bible occupies a unique and indispensable place. It is the fountainhead and source of the Christian faith. Anyone wishing to make progress as a disciple of Christ must be committed to regular reflection and meditation on the Scriptures. Blessed is the believer whose delight is in the Word of God, on which he or she "meditates day and night" (Psalm 1:1–2).

But we are not the first to read the Scriptures nor the first to meditate extensively on them. Christians of previous days also found strength and nourishment by meditating on the Word. And they recorded their wisdom for those who came after them in what we are in the habit of calling spiritual classics. Such classics thus have a way of sending their readers back to the Bible with deeper insight into the nature of the Christian faith and a greater desire to seek after Christ's glory and blessed presence.

—*Michael A.G. Haykin*